Robinson Locomotives

L N E R
5024

Robinson Locomotives

A Pictorial History by Brian Haresnape and Peter Rowledge

IA
LONDON
IAN ALLAN LTD

First published 1982

ISBN 0 7110 1151 6

Published by Ian Allan Ltd, Shepperton, Surrey;
and printed by Ian Allan Printing Ltd at their works
at Coombelands in Runnymede, England

Contents

Front endpaper: GCR Class 8B Atlantic No 260. *Ian Allan Library*

Rear endpaper: GCR Class 9N 4-6-2 No 450 on a down Local. *Real Photos*

Half title page: Vintage cameo of a Class 9N 4-6-2T on a Marylebone suburban working. *Ian Allan Library*

Left: Robinson's 2-8-0 freight locomotives had the distinction of being selected for military use in both world wars (a distinction shared with Sir William Stanier in World War 2). His design was built for war service in the period 1917-1920 and more than half of the 521 engines delivered ended up in peacetime LNER hands; passing to the ER of British Railways. Here BR No 63729 (LNER No 6309) is seen leaving York with an up mineral train on 10 April 1954. *Eric Treacy*

Preface

J. G. Robinson's claim to a place high among the ranks of immortal names of the great British steam engineers can be justified on two counts. Firstly, his locomotives were almost without exception reliable, simple and robust. Secondly they were also, and again almost without exception, superb works of art. If ever the term 'handsome is as handsome does' befitted steam locomotives, then Robinson's designs were the epitome of such a belief. The famous 'Jersey Lilies', as his Atlantics became known (after the equally famous Lily Langtry) were in particular quite magnificent in their appearance, and splendid in their performance.

It was however to be his 2-8-0 goods engine design for the Great Central that has today established his name and popularity in no uncertain terms. A straightforward and sturdy design, with no unnecessary frills of any description, some of these engines were to outlive many later types of goods engine, and were to be found in the most faraway places. What, one wonders, would Robinson have said, had he lived to see the day when his 2-8-0s were still working in Australia after the demise of steam on Britain's railways? (The story of how this came about is described in Section 14.) Some of the finest, and most important work achieved by these 2-8-0s was whilst in arduous military use, in both world wars.

I have been fortunate in having as co-author for this work, Peter Rowledge, who has made a close and detailed study of Robinson's locomotives for many years. His own writings on the 2-8-0 saga have been widely acclaimed, and the benefit of his researches can be found in this current work. The early Irish locomotives have also received the benefit of his attentions, and this serves to make the story all the more fascinating, as through them one can see Robinson as a young man gradually finding his feet as a locomotive engineer of true understanding.

No book dealing with any aspect of the Great

Below: The first of Robinson's passenger engines for the GCR appeared in 1901 and replaced Pollitt's 4-4-0s on the London Extension trains. The handsome original condition of the Class 11B is well captured in this photograph of No 1039 at the head of an up stopping train near Willesden Green. *Real Photographs*

fascinating story of the 'Last Main Line'.

As in the case of the earlier titles in this series of pictorial histories of the locomotive designs of Britain's steam engineers, I have attempted to select illustrations that will be of value to railway modellers in particular, by providing useful detailing. Indeed, a Robinson locomotive must prove to be a very real challenge to the modelmaker because of its subtle and curvaceous forms. The late J. N. Maskelyne in his book *Locomotives I have Known* published by Percival Marshall Ltd, points out that the chimney on the Atlantics had not a single straight line in it apart from the horizontals of the lip and flange. Herein lies the secret of Robinson's art. As George Dow reminds us in his aforementioned trilogy *Great Central*, Robinson himself once observed that: 'A chimney to a locomotive is like a hat to a man; the finishing touch'.

My sincere thanks are due, as always to A. B. Macleod of the Ian Allan Library, for much valuable advice and assistance. Other contributors and collectors are individually acknowledged with gratitude in the captions to the pictures themselves. The enthusiasm of those vintage photographers who stalked the Robinson engines as they raced through the green fields of Willesden and points north and whose pictures are reproduced herein, alone pays tribute to the fascination of Robinson's designs, in a manner I can but echo in words.

Brian Haresnape FRSA NDD
St Tropez, Var, France.
December 1980

Central Railway could possibly appear in print without the writer having consulted, at some stage, that *magnus opus* by George Dow, *Great Central*, published in three volumes by Ian Allan Ltd. Mr Dow's extensive researches are equalled only by his very readable presentation, and any reader of this current work is heartily recommended to delve further by courtesy of Mr Dow into the whole

Above: The hallmark of a Robinson design — his subtle and curvaceous chimney. The shape is clearly portrayed in this left hand view of Richmond Vale Railway (NSW) No 20. The lower gadget is one of Robinson's many patents, the superheater header discharge valve; the control rod from the footplate was carried inside the boiler handrail. *P. Ransome-Wallis*

Right: The typical footplate layout of a Robinson locomotive; showing the fittings on the faceplate and the right hand drive, which was standard on the GCR. Note the cans of oil on the tray above the firedoor, and the general impression of cleanliness and pride in the job. The locomotive is Class 11B 4-4-0 No 1035. The shapely curves of the cabside cutaway and driving wheel splashers echoed the chimney design. *W. Bradshaw courtesy V. R. Webster*

Introduction

John George Robinson, CBE, was born into a family which already had a railway background, in 1856. His father became District Locomotive Superintendent of the Great Western Railway at Bristol in 1876, and remained in the post until he retired in 1897. His older brother also worked for the GWR for over 50 years, and he retired in 1920, and he had a son (nephew of J. G.) who was destined to become District Locomotive Superintendent at Neasden LNER during World War 2. J. G. Robinson first served his apprenticeship at Swindon under both Joseph Armstrong and William Dean, and then left the GWR in 1884 to join the Waterford & Limerick, a rather small railway in Ireland, where he became assistant to H. Appleby, that line's Locomotive Superintendent. Only four years later he succeeded Appleby, and then Robinson had in his charge only 42 locomotives to run a railway of 280 miles. By 1900 he had added 33 new locomotives, of 12 classes, to bring the stock of the line up to 58. The next move took place in June 1900, when Robinson became Locomotive Superintendent of the Great Central Railway, with 791 locomotives and 504 miles of route.

It seems that the GCR Directors had set their sights on Robinson and had eliminated very quickly any other possible candidate with the result that only he was interviewed. The background story to this is apparently that S. W. Johnson of the Midland Railway, when touring in Ireland in the summer of 1899 had been very taken by the smartness of the Waterford, Limerick & Western engines and as a result had sought out Robinson to compliment him. In conversation he mentioned the impending retirement of Harry Pollitt from the Great Central and he apparently encouraged Robinson to apply for the job. Perhaps Robinson would not otherwise have thought of doing this as he was probably expecting to obtain a position on the new enlarged Great Southern & Western Railway, which was then taking steps to absorb the WLWR.

Robinson assumed his new post on the GCR at a time of rapidly growing traffic, some of which had for expediency to be handled by 54 locomotives borrowed from other railways. In the course of delivery, or on order, were the American built Moguls (Class 15) and six Pollitt singles (Class 13), also some 0-6-0 '9H' and 0-6-2T '9F'. Robinson set about building up the stock of the GCR with new designs and during the $22\frac{1}{2}$ years that he served the company at Gorton, no less than 25 new classes were introduced as shown in Table 1.

Table 1

1901	0-6-0	9J, 4-4-0 11B
1902	4-6-0	8, 0-8-0 8A
1903	4-4-2	8B, 4-6-0 8C, 4-4-2T 9K
1905	4-4-2	8D
1906	0-6-0T	5A, 4-4-2 8E, 4-6-0 8F, 4-6-0 8G
1907	0-8-4T	8H, 4-4-2T 9L
1911	2-8-0	8K, 4-6-2T 9N
1912	4-6-0	1
1913	4-6-0	1A, 4-4-0 11E
1914	2-6-4T	1B
1917	4-6-0	9P
1918	2-8-0	8M, 4-6-0 8N
1919	4-4-0	11F
1921	4-6-0	9Q

Below: All the grace of the outside cylinder engines of Robinson's first GCR design phase (1902-1906) is exemplified in this study of Class 8F 4-6-0 No 1099, built in 1906, and seen at the head of an up express between Harrow and Willesden. This class was in fact designed for fast goods and fish traffic, but was employed frequently on express passenger work until larger 4-6-0 types appeared. *Real Photographs*

Above: A direct comparison between the first phase of Robinson's GCR designs and the second phase (1911–1914), when new locomotives of the latter dates had with one exception two inside cylinders, and a rather massive appearance which lost something of the elegance of the earlier designs. Class 1 4-6-0 No 427 *City of London* stands at Neasden shed, with Class 8F 4-6-0 No 1108 in the right hand foreground. The photograph was evidently taken on the occasion of a railwayman's family visit, to judge from the poses and the small boy.
L&GRP courtesy David & Charles

A few variations were introduced by rebuilding, and these are described in the appropriate sections of the book. Following normal practice many older classes were rebuilt during this period, particularly by fitting new standard Belpaire boilers, but this aspect of his work is really outside the scope of this volume. Robinson and the GCR did not ignore the steam railmotor concept which enjoyed some popularity and three were built in 1904-5. The company also took the step of trying a petrol-electric engined vehicle. Both these experiments are described in Appendix 1.

The locomotive designs Robinson produced for the GCR can be placed into three broad categories,

Left: Of the classes of the middle phase of Robinson's GCR designs, when two inside cylinders were used the 'Director' class 4-4-0s undoubtedly gave the best performance. In latter days many worked on the Cheshire Lines Committee trains between Manchester Central and Chester Northgate, as is seen here with No 62662 (previously No 5508) at the head of the 12.52pm to Manchester, near Ashley in January 1952. The raking effect of the low winter sunlight emphasises the sheer mass of these engines. *D. J. Beaver*

Below left: The third and final phase of Robinson's GCR locomotive designs was in dramatic contrast to the earlier two. Use of four cylinders became the standard but in fact this produced no real improvement in performance and it resulted in his designs gaining a reputation for high coal consumption. LNER Class B3 No 6167 (formerly GCR Class 9P No 1167) heads the 5.0pm Marylebone-Manchester train past Willesden Green in 1933. Note the white painted roofs on all the carriages. *Real Photographs*

Below: In due course, Robinson's extremely shapely chimney design graced some other GCR locomotives with happy results, as seen on this Pollitt Class 11A (LNER Class D6) 4-4-0 No 877, photographed passing Halewood with a Liverpool-Manchester express on the Cheshire Lines route, in 1906. *LPC*

fairly well defined in their period of introduction. The first period between 1901 and 1906 saw the introduction of large, well balanced designs of engines, with two outside cylinders, although the few tank engines built were exceptions, because they were really his version of earlier Pollitt types. In this initial period there was some experimenting with compound locomotives, but this was not pursued once superheating became established. One speciality was the '8H' 0-8-4T of 1907. The second period, which began in 1911, saw the introduction of inside cylinder engines of quite massive proportions. Apart from the '9N' 4-6-2T and Classes 11E and 11F 'Director' 4-4-0s these were not so pleasing to the eye, nor so good in performance. The '8K' 2-8-0 which appeared in 1911 however, did have outside cylinders and this design really belonged to the first period, although in keeping with the second period an inside-cylinder version was also considered. This second period lasted until 1914 (although the last engines built to these designs did not appear until 1922, and the LNER built even more). The third and last period saw the introduction of larger boilered types, quite massive in appearance, which consisted of two classes with four cylinders and two with two outside cylinders; both (one a 2-8-0, the other a 4-6-0) being derivatives of the Class 8K 2-8-0 of 1911.

In retrospect and taking more than 60 years of development into consideration, it is probably true to say that the '8K' 2-8-0 has nowadays assumed an importance which it did not have at the time. Today the class is perhaps the one by which he is best remembered because it was chosen for large scale construction in 1917-20, when powerful goods locomotives were needed for military use in North-West Europe, during World War 1. Afterwards many of the type were sold to other railways, some even going as far as Australia and China. In World War 2 a number were requisitioned by the War Department and became a familiar sight at the eastern end of the Mediterranean. As a result Robinson's freight locomotives became more widespread than those of any other British railway company.

Unfortunately little is known of many of the variations that were put forward during proposals for some of the major classes. The Gorton drawing office register almost inevitably has the entry for the drawings concerned ruled out with a note

Left: Robinson reboilered a number of pre-1900 GCR classes, using his Belpaire type. An interesting rebuild with a larger boiler, was this 0-6-0 No 134 of Class 9H, which was constructed in 1902, at a time when pre-Robinson designs were still being delivered. In 1908 Robinson rebuilt it with his own Class 9J boiler and it lasted in this form until 1924, when it reverted back to its original boiler type and class. Whilst carrying the larger boiler it was allocated to Gorton, Stockport and Wrexham. *Real Photographs*

Below left: Robinson produced what was probably the most massive looking of any British single when he fitted a saturated boiler of the type used on his Class 11B 4-4-0s, to this final design by Pollitt, the Class 13 4-2-2, of which six were built for the London Extension. Only two of the class (known as 'Hell-fire Jacks') were actually delivered before Robinson arrived on the GCR, and the new CME was quick to realise that larger engines would be required for such duties. In 1911 he selected one of the Class, No 969 and subjected it to the rebuilding described above. The 7ft 9in driving wheels meant that the boiler had to be pitched very high upon the frames. The engine ran in this state until 1916.
W. H. Whitworth

'destroyed' against it. However some of the dates of proposals can be given where appropriate. The most interesting were those for a class of 2-10-2 heavy goods engine, for which two schemes were listed in July 1910, in addition to schemes for the eight coupled ideas which eventually saw the light of day. At a later stage a 2-10-2 was again considered, including a version proposed by the Baldwin Locomotive Works of Philadelphia, but nothing materialised and the GCR company met its needs by adding to existing types. Other ideas were for a Pacific and for a 2-6-0, and a scheme for a 0-10-2T design, intended for banking on the Worsborough incline, eventually materialised as the Gresley Garratt of 1925.

Until 1909 little attempt was made by Gorton to produce a range of standard boilers. Instead each of Robinson's classes had its own design, although this was often very similar to other GCR classes; Pollitt based designs were used for the earlier tank engines. Then however a standard range was introduced, which amounted to eight types. Nos 1 and 2 standard boilers were used on no less than 12 pre-Robinson classes, but on none of his own, whilst the No 3 type was used on two older classes as well as his 4-4-2T. These standard boilers were used as shown in Table 2.

For the classes listed in Table 2, all of which appeared before 1909, the standard boilers were replacements of the original type. Before then two classes of 4-6-0 had a common boiler, Classes 8C

This picture: A solitary rebuilding by Robinson produced this Class 90 0-6-2T No 771 of 1915; formerly a Pollitt Class 9F engine. He gave it a superheater boiler; side tanks extended forward to the front of the enlarged smokebox; enlarged bunker with coal rails (as on the Class 9N 4-6-2T); arched cab roof, and a pony truck instead of radial to allow the engine to traverse sharper curves. Screw couplings and carriage warming apparatus were also fitted, and these suggest that the engine was intended for passenger work, probably between Chester and Connah's Quay. Included in the 'N5' class by the LNER (who removed the superheater in 1930), the engine is seen here as BR No 69311, working a Chesterfield-Lincoln local goods train past Chipstone Sidings box (east of Warsop) in October 1950. The engine spent almost all of its time in this form at Gorton and Lincoln and rarely worked on a passenger train.
J. Cupit

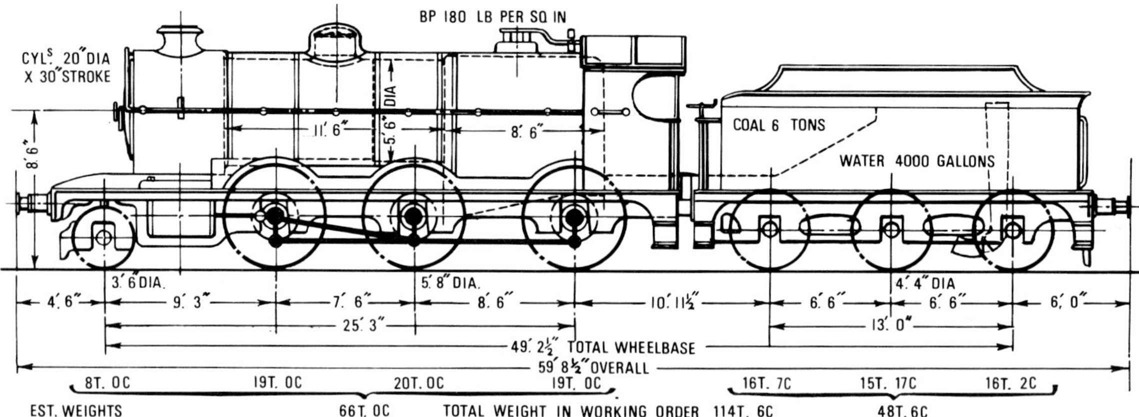

Above: One 'might have been' locomotive of the Robinson period was this outside cylinder 2-6-0. Other designs that did not leave the drawing board are known to have included one for an 0-10-2T banking engine; one for a Pacific for the Manchester-Sheffield route and at least two for a huge 2-10-2 freight engine intended for coal trains between the South Yorkshire coalfields and Immingham dock. This latter proposal was apparently further considered after a visit Robinson paid to the USA, from which stemmed an alternative proposal by the Baldwin Locomotive Works for a four-cylinder 2-10-2 (of typically American appearance,) for this specific GCR use in 1914.

and 8F (LNER B1 and B4), as did the 4-4-2T classes.

Table 2

Type	GCR classes	LNER classes
No 3	9K, 9L	C13, C14
No 4	9N, 11D	A5, D9
No 5	1B, 11E, 11F	L1, D10, D11
No 6	8D, 8E, 8K, 8H	C5, O4, S1
No 7	1, 1A, 9P, 9Q	B2, B8, B3, B7
No 8	8M, 8N	O5, B6

Only two sizes of tender was used with Robinson engines (with one special exception) and these had water capacities of 3,250 and 4,000gal capacity respectively. Water troughs were laid down at Charwelton and Killamarsh (72 and 156 miles from Marylebone), in 1905 and all tenders built subsequently had water pickup gear. The last few tenders of 1922-3 (plus the LNER built engines of 1924) which were attached to six 'Directors' and 18 '9Q' engines, were built with self-trimming bunkers. The tenders used are shown in Table 3.

Table 3

Capacity (gal)	Water Pick-up	Classes to which attached
3,250	No	8A, 9J
3,250	Yes	8, 8A, 9J
4,000	No	9J
4,000	Yes	1, 1A, 8, 8A, 8B, 8C, 8E, 8F 8G, 8K, 8M, 8N, 9J, 9P, 11B, 11C, 11D, 11E, 11F

NOTE: (All of these tenders carried 6 tons of coal)

Only a limited amount of changing of tenders occurred, in connection with providing older classes with water pick-up tenders in place of unfitted tenders. The special tender mentioned above is described in Section 14.

In the history of British steam locomotive engineering, Robinson's name is indelibly associated with the development of superheating. The first GCR engine to be superheated was an 0-6-0, Class 9J No 16 in 1909. This used Schmidt equipment, and was followed by a further 18 in 1911, after which Robinson's version came into use. Robinson's design had an improved method for fitting the elements to the header, to make steam tight joints. In these early days of superheating various devices were added to counteract the effects created by running with the regulator closed and with the elements empty of steam. Robinson patented some of these gadgets, the first being a draught retarder which consisted of a series of small steam nozzles which were placed in the smokebox end of the flue tubes, the steam supply being connected to the blower so that, when it was opened, just enough steam was directed into the flues to destroy the draught in them and protect the empty superheater elements. This gadget was later replaced by a combined blower and circulating valve. This valve allowed a small amount of steam to pass through the elements when the regulator was closed, in addition to its normal blower action. To prevent

unintended movement of the engine there had to be a header discharge valve as well, and this was opened by a rod passing alongside the boiler connected to the regulator. All this gadgetry was gradually replaced by Gresley's anti-vacuum valve from 1923 onwards; this was a much simpler device which opened, when steam pressure in the elements dropped to admit air, as it was found that there was no risk in burning the elements at the firebox end. Piston tailrods were another feature associated with the Robinson superheater engines, and these were gradually dispensed with by Gresley in LNER days.

Many Robinson engines were fitted with ash ejectors whereby live steam, admitted to the smokebox, disturbed the ash and ejected it through the chimney. This device, confined to the larger engines, were not displaced very rapidly by the LNER and survived on many engines to the post-World War 2 years. Other Robinson patents were his own form of top feed, introduced in 1914, which later failed to find favour with the LNER, and

Above: Although some Robinson engines have earned justified fame for their wanderings to various parts of the world, their own homeground remained a veritable Robinson stronghold throughout LNER and early BR days. Until electrification in 1954, the Worsborough incline was the scene of a daily battle for adhesion, with every train requiring assistance on its long 1 in 40 gradient between Barnsley and Penistone. Just two of the many engines involved are seen here, in April 1947, 2-8-0 No 3888 (ex-No 6637) with the tender still lettered with the wartime NE, and 'Pom-Pom' 0-6-0 No 4400 (ex No 5285). *H. C. Casserley*

Below: Of all Robinson's classes for the GCR it was his Atlantics which were held in the greatest affection and esteem by the enthusiasts of the day. The 'Jersey Lilies', as they were fondly known, had a design which was bold but neat and graceful. Unhappily when the original chimney design wore out the LNER replaced it with a rather less elegant type, as seen here on No 5263, photographed at Willesden Green on an up excursion in 1931, with six of the famous 'Barnum' coaches in the formation. The engine retains its right hand drive and four enclosed safety valves. *Real Photographs*

Left: Just about as far afield as an earthbound locomotive can get from Gorton, one of the ex-'Ministry of Munitions' engines of World War 1 shunts at the Hexham exchange sidings of the Richmond Vale Railway in February 1966. The engine portrayed started life as ROD No 2002 (Richmond Rly No 22) built at Gorton in 1918. An odd distinction befell the three ex GCR-built engines that worked on this line — namely that they were the last *standard* gauge examples of the countless thousands of steam locomotives built by the workshops of Britain's former railway companies to remain in ordinary commercial service, as opposed to the engines built by the various outside contractors in Great Britain. *R. T. Horne*

also the 'Intensifor' lubricator, a form of sight-feed lubricator, which was replaced by other types from the mid-1930s onwards. The GCR conducted experiments with a train control device in the London area known as 'Reliostop' in 1919-21 for

Below: Forlorn and far from home, on the left stand six of the Robinson 2-8-0 engines that went to Australia, as they await scrapping at Hexham (NSW) in 1970. The two engines in the right hand foreground are Kitson-built 2-8-2Ts and a similarity between certain features of the two types cannot go unnoticed! *Leon Oberg*

which several of the '9N' 4-6-2T and some of the 4-6-0 engines were fitted. Also, in addition to the use of oil during the coal strike of 1921, the GCR experimented with pulverised coal and a mixture of coal and oil as described in Section 14.

Apart from changes of boiler type, the most obvious alterations to the appearance of Robinson's engines were those created by the later reduction in the height of the locomotives, to conform to the LNER standard loading gauge. The GCR had been more generous in that respect than several other constituents of the new LNER system. This reduction was achieved by fitting new lower chimneys and dome covers. The chimney used on several classes were regarded as particularly ugly by many enthusiasts and was the subject of much criticism, being known as the 'flower pot' type. With the flattened dome cover this 'flower pot' chimney certainly detracted in no small way from the appearance of Robinson's engines. Later a more attractive shape of chimney was produced and this abated the outcry. In addition, on some classes, the cab roof and whistle had to be altered to conform to the reduced loading gauge.

When the Great Central Railway became part of the LNER in the 1923 Amalgamation, Robinson was the senior of all the CME's of the constituent companies, and the LNER directors accordingly offered him the same post in the new company. He chose to decline their offer, and lived on in retirement until 1943. The new CME was H. N. Gresley from the Great Northern Railway. Gresley admired Robinson's work and used certain details for his own designs, as well as ordering further Robinson engines for LNER use. Examples of Robinson's engines were destined to survive until the end of steam on British Railways. What finer tribute could be found.

J. W. P. Rowledge, C.Eng, M.I. Mech E.
London
December 1980

Early Days in Ireland
SECTION 1

Locomotives for the Waterford & Limerick Railway 1884–1900

When Robinson arrived at Limerick in 1884 the railway comprised a main line from Waterford to Limerick plus a long branch to Tuam in Co Galway, another to Tralee in Co Kerry and some shorter branches. The major extension of 1893-5 took the WLR northwards to reach Sligo (by running powers over the Midland Great Western Railway for the last six miles) and then the company changed its name to the Waterford, Limerick & Western Railway.

The 42 engines extant in 1884 were indeed a very mixed collection, even including a couple dating back to 1848-9. But from that time, until 1888, only three new engines were obtained to replace older stock. These were 4-4-0 Nos 9 *Garryowen* and 12 *Earl of Bessborough*, and 0-6-0 No 24 *Sarsfield,* all delivered in 1886.

The details of each of Robinson's Irish locomotives are given in Table 4; it will be noted that they were all named.

Passenger Tender Locomotives

With the two 1886 passenger engines, the 4-4-0 wheel arrangement was introduced to the railway, but when it was decided to obtain further motive power the engines produced were 2-4-0s, losing the bogie at some stage in designing. In fact the specification called for a copy of No 12 (built by the Vulcan Foundry) but Dubs got the contract and produced a new version of No 9 which they had supplied! In all eight were built in 1889-94, as listed in Table 4; and the class was regarded as the most attractive of Robinson's engines in Ireland. One lasted until 1959 and was the longest lived of all Robinson's engines in public service, having worked for no less than 66 years.

The final main line passenger engines obtained by the WLWR were the three 4-4-0 Nos 53-5 of 1896-7, which were a bogie version of the Dubs 2-4-0, supplied by Kitson. No 53 was named in honour of the Jubilee years of the company, in 1896. Unlike the 2-4-0s all three lasted until the 1925 formation of the Great Southern Railways and two were rebuilt and lasted until 1949.

Passenger Tank Locomotives

The first passenger tank engines obtained by the

Left: Only six locomotives were constructed by the Limerick works of the W&LR; the first in 1888 and the last in 1899. Illustrated is Robinson's first engine, No 7 (seen here as GS&WR No 226), originally named *Progress* and later renamed *Wasp*. Apart from loss of the nameplates it appears to be little altered in this picture except that it has acquired a different chimney and dome from the GS&WR. Very few dimensions are known (see table five).
Real Photographs

Below left: The 2-4-0 engines were widely regarded as the prettiest of Robinson's designs for Ireland, and they must have looked exceedingly smart in the W&LR livery of crimson lake with black lining, edged with yellow and fine red lines. The chimney cap, dome cover, nameplate and beading were all highly polished. Illustrated is No 47 *Carrick Castle*, built by Dubs in 1894.
Real Photographs

Above right: Another view of No 291, taken in its final years at Limerick. During raw material shortages in World War 2, the GSR had to recover the white metal numberplates, and these were replaced by painted numerals. Of the 58 engines handed over by the WLWR in 1901, this was the last to survive; outlasting its original owners by no less than 58 years. *Real Photographs*

Below right: The introduction of a couple of 2-4-2T engines in 1891 heralded a new policy of using tank engines on the branch lines of the W&LR, and this pair spent their early years on the Limerick to Tralee and Fenit branch trains. W&LR No 13 (GS&WR No 266) is shown here as Cork & Macroon Direct Railway No 6, after sale in 1914. The engine is still virtually in original condition apart from the removal of the toolbox from the bunker to a new position on the left side of the smokebox, and the substitution of fluted for plain coupling rods.
Real Photographs

Left: Four out of the eight 2-4-0 engines survived into Great Southern Railway ownership, and were fitted with new boilers in 1924-26; at the same time receiving typical Inchicore fittings and cab. GSR No 291 (ex-W&LR No 44 *Nephin*) spent some years working on the former Midland Great Western Railway branch from Athymon Junction to Loughrea, and is depicted on the afternoon branch working, running down the main line to Galway and back to change engines.

Below: After it was acquired by the GS&WR, to become their No 267, the second 2-4-2T — No 14 of the W&LR — carried an old fashioned type of smokebox with a double door (that could hardly have been airtight) of a design favoured by Inchicore works throughout the nineteenth century. It also had a built-up chimney. No 267 joined the ranks of the great variety of engines that were sent to work on the Dublin suburban services after the 1925 Amalgamation, when so many of the original Dublin & South Eastern locomotives were condemned. However, it finished its days supplying steam for washing-out at Broadstone shed in Dublin.
Real Photographs

company appeared in 1891 and were a tank version of a series of Vulcan Foundry 2-4-0s supplied in 1874-82. The GSWR sold the first of the pair in 1914 but it came into GSR stock in 1925. Instead of reverting to its GSWR number of 266 it became No 491. The other engine was altered by the GSWR, getting a very old-fashioned type of smokebox with double folding doors. This engine was sent in 1925 to help out with Dublin suburban services and after withdrawal in 1935 it survived for several years as a stationary boiler at Broadstone engine shed. The next two engines were built at Limerick and were replacements of old 0-4-2 and are sometimes recorded as rebuildings of those engines. The first of the pair, No 3 of 1892 retained the same wheel arrangement, but the second, No 15 of 1894 was somewhat larger, having a rear bogie (which had been taken from 4-4-0 No 12 when it was converted to a 2-4-0 the same year). The 0-4-2T was for years the Killaloe branch engine, but No 15 appears always to have worked from Limerick; both lasting until 1912.

When the northward extension of the railway took place in 1894-5 tank engines were selected instead of tender engines, which would have been

Above right: 0-4-2T No 3 *Zetland* (named after the then Lord Lieutenant of Ireland) was delivered in 1892. The design exhibits all the signs of the straightforward approach that Robinson was developing, but details are sadly lacking and the only known dimensions are given in Table five. In its relatively short life of 20 years the engine appears to have worked only on the Killaloe branch. *L&GRP courtesy David & Charles*

Centre right: The eight Dubs and Kitson built 0-6-0 engines of 1893-1900 were the main line goods power of the WLWR, at the end of its separate existence. The first of the class, No 45 *Colleen Bawn* (GS&WR No 233) is seen at Waterford. Although these engines carried lined-out livery, they had a painted dome cover and a plain chimney of the shape that was to become characteristic of Robinson. *Real Photographs*

Below: The front end details, complete with smokebox wingplates, are more apparent in this view of another Dubs engine, No 49 *Dreadnought* (GS&WR No 235) seen here at Listowel in September 1901. Note the square-shaped lamps and brackets. The GS&WR replaced the square brackets on the engines, but not on the tenders, and the latter survived as such until the demise of steam in Eire. *LCGB/Ken Nunn collection*

Above: The last new engine delivered to the WLWR, in 1900, was 0-6-0 No 2 *Shannon* (GS&WR No 222) which introduced the Belpaire boiler to the major Irish railways. (The Schull and Skibbereen narrow gauge line had one as early as 1888). By the time that *Shannon* arrived, the livery for goods engines was black, retaining the lining-out. The Kitson engines of 1897-1900 had a slightly larger boiler but were otherwise very similar to the Dubs version. *LPC*

Below: One of the last pair of engines ordered by the WLWR, 0-6-0 No 11 *Samson*, built by Kitson. It is seen here in original livery but in Midland Great Western Railway guise. The MGWR oval numberplate (142) is surrounded by the rectangular lining which surrounded the original WLWR plate, and the new name *Athenry* is affixed over the original nameplate. *H. Fayle*

Left: Six of the goods engines survived the Amalgamation of 1925, and were rebuilt in the period 1923-27 with new boilers and Inchicore pattern cabs. Another change was to vacuum braking for the engine instead of the combination steam brake which had been standard on the WLWR. Unlike the GS&WR, the WLWR engines were right hand drive, and they retained this feature when rebuilt. No 239 (old No 58) is seen at Athenry, where the long branch from Limerick to Sligo crosses the MGWR Dublin-Galway main line. Unlike some former WLWR engines, this class had only limited work elsewhere in GSR days; being divided between Limerick and Waterford. *Real Photographs*

more suited for the run of 145 miles to Sligo. The first two were Kitson's version of the 1891 2-4-2T being 0-4-4T Nos 51/2; one was condemned in 1910 but the other lasted until 1954 and became well known as the Foynes branch engine. Another four came in 1896-7 but they were of the 4-4-2T wheel arrangement. Originally these were very attractive engines but their appearance was later somewhat marred because the GSR altered them and fitted larger side tanks. They moved further afield and after some use on Dublin suburban trains they all finished up at Cork on the Bandon section; No 269 (WLWR No 16) was the last Robinson tank engine in Ireland. The final passenger tank was No 27 and this was in most respects a copy of Nos 51/52. Like most of the WLWR engines which survived World War 1 No 27 was rebuilt, although not altered so much as some of the others. It never returned to Limerick, as it proved to be one of the most successful of the great variety of the engines

Right: No 15 *Roxborough* was the second tank engine to be built at Limerick, and only certain dimensions were the same as its predecessor. In particular it had a larger bunker and a rear bogie, making it an 0-4-4T. The side tanks were shorter. The photograph was taken adjacent to the works and the WLWR engine shed, at Limerick. *Real Photographs*

22

Above: It was the extension northward from Tuam to Sligo that warranted the greatest increase in locomotive stock during the Robinson era, and despite its length of 145 miles from Limerick, the passenger trains were normally worked by tank engines. Pictured in September 1898 is No 52 *Brian Boru* (later GS&WR No 295) and this rather handsome engine displays the special headcode carried by WLWR trains when running over the MGWR metals between Coollooney and Sligo. The shine on the dome cover is quite remarkable — what a labour of love must have been involved in keeping it in such a brilliant state! *LCGB/Ken Nunn collection*

Below: Old No 52 (GS&WR No 295) is seen here again, after rebuilding in 1926 with larger side tanks. Changes were also made to the smokebox and chimney and the bunker, but unlike the other rebuilt WLWR engines the steam brake was retained. This engine spent its entire working life in the the Limerick area, latterly associated with the Foynes branch train which took no less than 2h 26min to cover the $26\frac{3}{4}$-mile journey, and 15min longer on the return! It is related that a lone enthusiast was the occasional passenger for this snail's pace marathon; travelling in a solitary ancient six-wheeler. *B. Waters*

Above: For the Claremorris to Sligo extension of 1895 Robinson specified four 4-4-2T engines, which were delivered in 1896-97. In practice they were also used on the Tralee line. When new they were subjected to an inspection by the Irish Board of Works, which had sponsored the construction of the line northwards from Claremorris. No 16 is seen at Limerick in September 1900. The sense of style and elegance of Robinson's later engines can be seen here in embryonic form. No 16 *Rocklands* became No 269 on the GS&WR list. *LCGB/Ken Nunn collection*

Left: The GSR found the 4-4-2Ts useful elsewhere, including the Dublin suburban traffic, but by 1940 all of them were at Cork, working on the former Cork, Bandon & South Coast lines. No 274 (originally No 21 *Blarney Castle*) is seen, after rebuilding, approaching Skibbereen with a Baltimore train in July 1938. No 274 spent its last few years at Dublin, but the others remained on the CB&SCR section, until the class was withdrawn in the period 1949-57. *H. C. Casserley*

used on the Dublin area suburban trains of the GSR, but for its final years it worked from Broadstone shed.

Goods Tender Engines

The earliest of Robinson's goods engines were in theory reconstructions of older locomotives but were in reality new. No 7 is known to have had plates on the frames inscribed 'W&LR Company, Builders, Limerick'. Limerick works was not well enough equipped to entirely manufacture these engines, and therefore major parts, such as the frames and boilers were supplied by outside locomotive builders. These engines had boilers closely copied from the old Sharp Stewart engines that they replaced, even to the extent of having the outdated raised firebox.

Ten more 0-6-0s were built to W&LR/WLWR orders and these may be regarded as the standard goods engines existing at the end of the company's existence. The first four came from Dubs in 1893-5, followed by three from Kitson in 1897. They were a goods version of Robinson's 2-4-0

engines, but the 1897 locomotives had a bigger boiler and several detail alterations. The final engine delivered to the WLWR was No 2 of 1900 and this modified version introduced the Belpaire boiler to the major Irish railways, but otherwise it was like the 1897 locomotives. Two more were ordered and were ready for delivery in the autumn of 1900, but due to the impending amalgamation with the GSWR the makers made enquiries about

Above: The original grace and style of Robinson's 4-4-2T design was somewhat disfigured by the rebuilding they underwent in 1924-26, when they received larger side tanks and bunker, and chimney. No 270 (originally No 17 *Faugh-a-Ballagh*) was photographed at Inchicore works after an overhaul; about 1946. *R. N. Clements*

Below: A view of the smart-looking 4-4-0 No 53, taken at Limerick in September 1900. After they were displaced by larger GS&WR engines they remained at Waterford and Limerick, working secondary trains. Latterly they were most often to be seen on the Sligo line. *LCGB/Ken Nunn collection*

Right: Robinson's final main line passenger engines for the WL&WR were a bogie version of the Dubs 2-4-0. Illustrated is No 53 *Jubilee*, built by Kitson in 1896. The principal duties for the class were the Limerick to Waterford mail and boat trains, which also conveyed perishable traffic. Many of the components of these three 4-4-0s were standard with the 0-6-0 goods engines; including the boiler and the motion. By this time Robinson had abandoned the use of smokebox wingplates; thereby giving a more modern appearance to the front end. Note the rerailing jack prominently carried on the running plate, above the bogie. *LPC*

the way they would be paid. At first the company said that they intended to pay by instalments but they very quickly asked the makers to find other purchasers. So it was that in November 1900 the GSWR made an offer which was much less than the contract price. Despite this, for some reason it was not accepted, but in January 1901 the same sum was accepted from the Midland Great Western Railway and the GSWR was told that it had made its offer too late. These engine then became MGWR Nos 141 *Limerick* and 142 *Athenry*. Several of these engines were rebuilt by the GSR and some lasted until 1949-51, as listed in Table 4.

The known dimensions for Robinson's Irish locomotives are detailed in Table 5; in some cases these are incomplete.

Table 4

Robinson Locomotives in Ireland

No	Name	Type	Date	Maker	GSWR No	Withdrawn
7	*Progress**	0-6-0	1888	WLR	226	1905
10	*Sir James*	2-4-0	1889	Dubs	263	1907
6	*Ant*	0-6-0	1890	WLR	225	1907
22	*Era*	2-4-0	1890	Dubs	275	1913
13	*Derry Castle*	2-4-2T	1891	Vulcan Foundry	266	1933†
14	*Lough Derg*	2-4-2T	1891	Vulcan Foundry	267	1935
3	*Zetland*	0-4-2T	1892	WLR	260	1912
20	*Galteemore*	2-4-0	1892	Dubs	273	1909
23	*Slieve-na-Mon*	2-4-0	1892	Dubs	276	1949
5	*Bee*	0-6-0	1893	WLR	224	1909
43	*Knockma*	2-4-0	1893	Dubs	290	1951
44	*Nephin*	2-4-0	1893	Dubs	291	1959
45	*Colleen Bawn*	0-6-0	1893	Dubs	233	1919
46	*Erin-go-Bragh*	0-6-0	1893	Dubs	234	1911
15	*Roxborough*	0-4-4T	1894	WLR	268	1912
47	*Carrick Castle*	2-4-0	1894	Dubs	292	1913
48	*Granston*	2-4-0	1894	Dubs	293	1954
49	*Dreadnought*	0-6-0	1895	Dubs	235	1928
50	*Hercules*	0-6-0	1895	Dubs	236	1951
51	*Castle Hackett*	0-4-4T	1895	Kitson	294	1910
52	*Brian Boru*	0-4-4T	1895	Kitson	295	1954
16	*Rocklands*	4-4-2T	1896	Kitson	269	1957
17	*Faugh-a-Ballagh*	4-4-2T	1896	Kitson	270	1949
53	*Jubilee*	4-4-0	1896	Kitson	296	1949
54	*Killemnee*	4-4-0	1896	Kitson	297	1928
18	*Geraldine*	4-4-2T	1897	Kitson	271	1949
21	*Blarney Castle*	4-4-2T	1897	Kitson	274	1949
55	*Bernard*	4-4-0	1897	Kitson	298	1949
56	*Thunderer*	0-6-0	1897	Kitson	237	1951
57	*Cyclops*	0-6-0	1897	Kitson	238	1934
58	*Goliath*	0-6-0	1897	Kitson	239	1949
27	*Thomond*	0-4-4T	1899	WLWR	279	1953
2	*Shannon*	0-6-0	1900	Kitson	222	1949
(4	*Shamrock*)	0-6-0	1900	Kitson	‡	1929
(11	*Samson*)	0-6-0	1900	Kitson	‡	1950

FOOTNOTES TO TABLE
*Later renamed *Wasp*.
† Sold to Cork & Macroom Direct Railway (No 6) in 1914 and became Great Southern Railways No 491 in 1925.
‡ Delivered to Midland Great Western Railway, Nos 141 *Limerick* and 142 *Athenry* (GSR Nos 233 and 234).

Right: Two of the three 4-4-0s, Nos 296/8 (old Nos 53/5) were rebuilt by Inchicore in 1924/29 respectively. The rebuilding used the same boiler as the 2-4-0 and 0-6-0 classes, with the substitution of a typical Inchicore built-up chimney and square cab 'spectacles' for the original round type. *Real Photographs*

Below right: The last WLWR passenger tank engine, built at Limerick in 1899, was a reversion to the 0-4-4T type, being a fairly close copy of the Kitson engines of 1895. This was No 27 *Thomond* which became GS&WR No 279. Rebuilding by the GSR in 1925 did not alter the appearance much (although a new boiler was provided) except for the chimney style; for some reason the original round cab windows were retained. After rebuilding the engine never returned to Limerick, proving useful for some years on Dublin suburban trains, followed by long spells at Bagenalstown and then Broadstone, Dublin.

TABLE 5

Locomotive Dimensions (as built)

Type	Nos	GSR class	Cylinder inches	Ldg ft	in	Wheels cpld ft	in	Trg ft	in	Boiler pressure lb/sq in	Heating tubes sq ft	Surface firebox sq ft	Grate area sq ft	Coal ton	Water gal	Engine weight ton	cwt	Tender weight ton	cwt
2-4-0	10, 22, 20/3, 43/4/7/ 8	276	17×24	4	0	6	0			160	991	107	17¾	2½	2,000	36	9	22	11
2-4-2T	13/4	267	16×24	3	6	5	6	3	6	150	806	88	15	2	1,200	45	0		
0-6-0	45/6/ 9, 50	235	17×24			5	1½			150	991	107	17¾	3¼	1,864	36	12		
0-4-4T	51/2	295	16×24			5	6	3	6	150	780	88	15	1½	1,000	43	0		
4-4-2T	16-8,21	269	16×24	3	6	5	6	3	6	150	780	88	15	1¾	1,040	46	19		
4-4-0	53-5	296	17×24	3	6	6	0			150	887	107	17¾	4	2,000	40	12	27	8
0-6-0	56-8	222	17×24			5	2			150	887	107	17¾	4	2,000	38	13	27	8
0-6-0	2 and MGWR 141/2	222	17×24			5	2			150	873	108	17¾	4	2,000	38	13	27	8
0-4-4T	27	279	16×24			5	4	3	6	150	808	88	15½	2½	1,200	49	19		
0-6-0	5/6/7		16×24			4	7												
0-4-2T	3		16×24			4	7												
0-4-4T	15		16×24			4	7												

Locomotives for the Great Central Railway and Military Use

SECTION 2

GCR Class 9J, LNER Class J11, J11/3*, BR Class 3F
0-6-0 Goods Engines
Introduced: 1901, 1942*
Total: 174 (31 J11/3*)

Robinson's first class for the GCR proved to be the most numerous produced in the company's time, although it was later to be far exceeded in number, when the LNER purchased surplus Robinson 2-8-0 War Department engines in 1923-7. Very quickly they became known as 'Pom-Poms' because of their sharp exhaust which was likened to the sound of a quick firing gun of a sort that had been used in the recent Boer War. They were an enlargement of Pollitt's '9H' class of 1896-1902, of which no less than 40 had been delivered after Robinson's arrival at Gorton. The major difference was the size of the boiler and '9H' No 134, which was fitted with this boiler in 1908 (becoming '9M' class), was included in the same class by the LNER until it reverted to its original form in 1924 when it then joined the 'J10' class. All but one of the class were built with saturated boilers and slide valves, the exception being No 16 of 1909 which had a Schmidt superheater and 8in piston valves. A non-standard feature of this engine was the longer front end, due to the piston tail rods, and this was retained until 1927. Superheating of the bulk of the class was started in 1913 and all were fitted by 1946.

Beginning in 1942 the LNER and later British Railways rebuilt 31 engines as Class J11/3 with new cylinders, having piston valves; no more were altered after 1953. In fact this version was selected as a standard LNER type for postwar construction, it being announced that 115 were to be built in the 1945-50 programme; they would have had round top fireboxes had they materialised.

Below: Superheated version of GCR Class 9J 0-6-0, with solid coal rail, or guard, on tender and four column safety valves enclosed in casing.

Above right: Class 9J 0-6-0 No 980, built by Neilson Reid & Co in 1901; seen during smokebox cleaning. Slender version of Robinson chimney, and twin column Ramsbottom safety valves. Original pattern tender, with two open coal rails, of 3,250gal capacity.
Ian Allan Library

Below right: A 'Pom-pom' at the head of a goods near Leicester. Wider version of Robinson chimney, and four column Ramsbottom safety valves. Tender with four open coal rails and water pick-up apparatus
Ian Allan Library

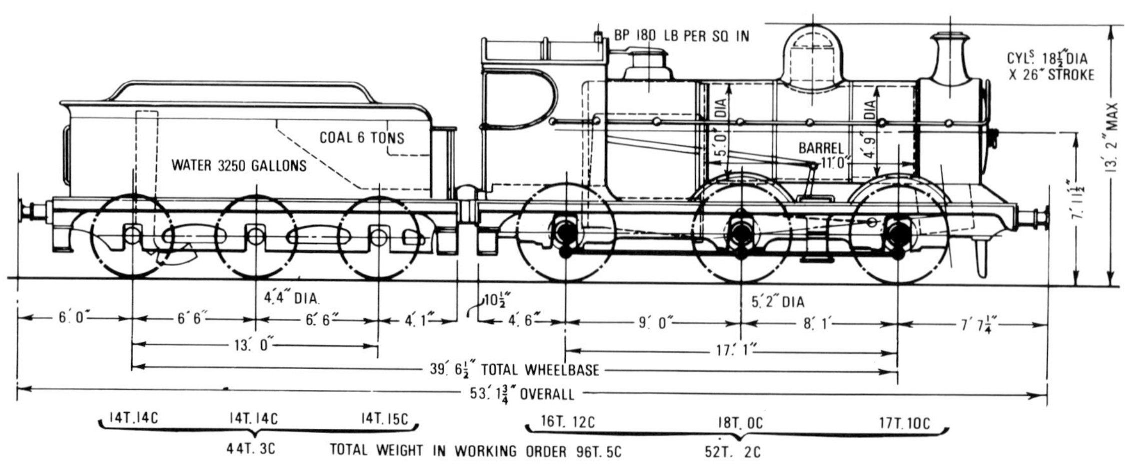

The first 40 engines had 3,250gal tenders without water pick-up, the next 66 of 1902-4 had the same type but with pick-up gear fitted, while the remaining 68 had the larger 4000gal tender, also with pick-up gear; however in 1939 the process of replacing these latter tenders by others not fitted began, the displaced tenders passing to other former GCR classes.

The engines were built as follows (GCR numbers):

Nos 973-94	Neilson, Reid	1901
Nos 995-1012	Neilson, Reid	1902
Nos 1043-51	Neilson, Reid	1902
Nos 198, 201/3/5/6/9/10/1/4/5	Beyer, Peacock	1903
Nos 216/8/9/21-31/4	Beyer, Peacock	1904
Nos 177/97, 202	Gorton	1903
Nos 204/7/8/17/20/32/3/40/1	Gorton	1904
Nos 235-9/42-50/2	Vulcan Foundry	1904
Nos 253-7	Yorkshire Engine Co	1904
Nos 1078-82	Yorkshire Engine Co	1905
Nos 1115-9	Yorkshire Engine Co	1906
Nos 281/2	Gorton	1906
Nos 283-99, 300-9/11-8	Gorton	1907
Nos 319/20/2-30	Gorton	1908
No 16	Gorton	1909
Nos 947-55	Gorton	1910

In the LNER 1946 renumbering the class became Nos 4280-4453 in the order given above.

In World War 1 18 were loaned to the Railway Operating Division (ROD), in 1917 and all were eventually returned safely from France in 1919. At the formation of the LNER 92 of the class were shared between Woodford, Immingham and Gorton, the rest being scattered in smaller numbers at the other principal GCR sheds. Apart from a few sent to former GER sheds in 1927 for a short while, and six sent in 1936 to the Midland & Great Northern Joint line, they were confined to former GCR and Cheshire Lines sheds, with a minor exception of two at Louth (ex-Great Northern Railway). Although found suitable for passenger work it was not until their latter years that they were so used in quantity and generally the piston valve engines were found to be slightly faster and freer engines.

Last of class withdrawn: '9J' 64329, 64445 (8/1962) 'J11/3' 64354 (10/1962)
None preserved:

The basic dimensions of the class in GCR days were as follows:

	As built	Superheated
Heating surface, tubes:		
Large and small (sq ft):	1,296	1,128
Firebox (sq ft):	130	130
Total (evaporative) (sq ft):	1,426	1,258
Superheater (sq ft):	—	139
Superheater elements:	—	18
Combined heating surfaces (sq ft):	1,426	1,397
Grate area (sq ft):	19	19
Tractive effort (lbs at 85% BP):	21,959	21,959

Below: Heading a Sheffield-Cleethorpes excursion train composed of ancient Manchester, Sheffield and Lincolnshire Railway six-wheeled stock in July 1919, is No 1116 with later type tender with solid coal guards and 4,000gal capacity. *P. Ransome-Wallis*

Left: The first GCR engine to be superheated was No 16 of the '9J' class, built in 1909 with a Schmidt superheater. In 1913 the class generally began to receive superheaters (a process which dragged on until 1946!). One difference was that No 16 had piston valves, whereas slide valves were retained on the rest (except those converted to Class J11/3 from 1942 onwards). No 16 is seen here as LNER No 5016. It received slide valve cylinders in 1927. Detail changes include plated coal rails on tender, plain LNER chimney and Gresley type snifting valve behind chimney. *Photomatic*

Centre left: Class J11/3, with higher-pitched superheated boiler and long travel valves (note altered layout below smokebox) and with modified style dome cover and chimney, to suit loading gauge. No 64427 was photographed on shed at Langwith. Edward Thompson selected the 'J11s' as a postwar standard class for the LNER, in preference to the Gresley Class J39. He intended to replace the Belpaire boiler with a round-topped version, but this was never implemented. *J. Davenport*

Below: In LNER and BR days the 'Pom-poms' were classified as 'J11'. A sub classification was 'J11/3' given to 31 engines rebuilt from 1942 onwards with long travel valves and higher-pitched superheated boiler. Other sub classifications referred to tender types, height of boiler mountings and superheating. No 64286 is seen here approaching Lincoln at the head of an excursion train, in July 1951. Tall plain LNER chimney and low dome.
P. H. Wells

GCR Class 11B, 11C & 11D, LNER Class D9, BR Class 2P
4-4-0 Passenger Engines
Introduced: 1901
Total: 40

At the turn of the century there seemed to be a never ending demand for larger and larger passenger engines, as trains got heavier as a result of more extensive demands for better passenger facilities; particularly restaurant car services. The GCR, under its determined General Manager, Sam Fay, made considerable efforts to provide competitive fast trains on its London extension. For these trains Robinson soon produced an engine larger than the existing types of his predecessors which really belonged to the Victorian size of trains, although they had been very capable while loads were limited. The first duties of the new engines, Class 11B, were in fact on Manchester to Hull trains, but they soon found their way on to London trains, and through workings to both the GWR and LSWR via Banbury were part of their daily work. However it was on the Cheshire lines that the class was best known, and the majority worked in that area, once displaced by even larger engines on the London extension.

Capable and popular though they were, it was evident that a bigger boiler would improve the class, so in 1907 Nos 107 and 110 were fitted with a larger diameter boiler having a longer firebox, and these then became Class 11C. The next rebuilding was that of No 1026 in 1910, having a boiler with the same diameter barrel as Nos 107 and 110, but the shorter firebox of the original type. In this form the engine became Class 11D. Then in 1913 this same boiler, but fitted with a superheater, was used for the general conversion of the class and by 1926 all were altered to the '11D' version, the '11C' variety disappearing in 1923-4 with the conversion of Nos 104 and 110.

Four were named, three after royalty, the other after the company's chairman, the nameplates of this latter engine being removed in 1913, when the name was bestowed on a new engine (see section 17).

The 40 engines of this class were built as follows:

Nos 1013-7	Sharp, Stewart	1901
Nos 1018-37	Sharp, Stewart	1902
Nos 1038-42	Sharp, Stewart	1903
Nos 104-13	Vulcan Foundry	1904

In LNER ownership the engines become Nos 6013-6042 and 5104-5113, in the same order. The 1946 LNER renumbering altered Nos 6013-9/21/3-7/9-41, 5104-9/11 to 2300-33, but Nos 6025/32/6/9, 5104/5 were withdrawn unaltered.

Below right: Apart from the fitting of a four column safety valve, in place of the original two column version, Class 11B 4-4-0 No 1030, still in original state, works an up semi-fast from Nottingham to Marylebone. The extremely varied collection of rolling stock includes three six-wheelers at the leading end, and serves as a reminder that the beginning of the 20th century witnessed a progressive increase in the size and weight of passenger carriages, which in turn led to demands for larger passenger engines to haul them. *V. R. Webster*

Below: GCR Class 11D (rebuild), LNER Class D9 4-4-0 passenger engines.

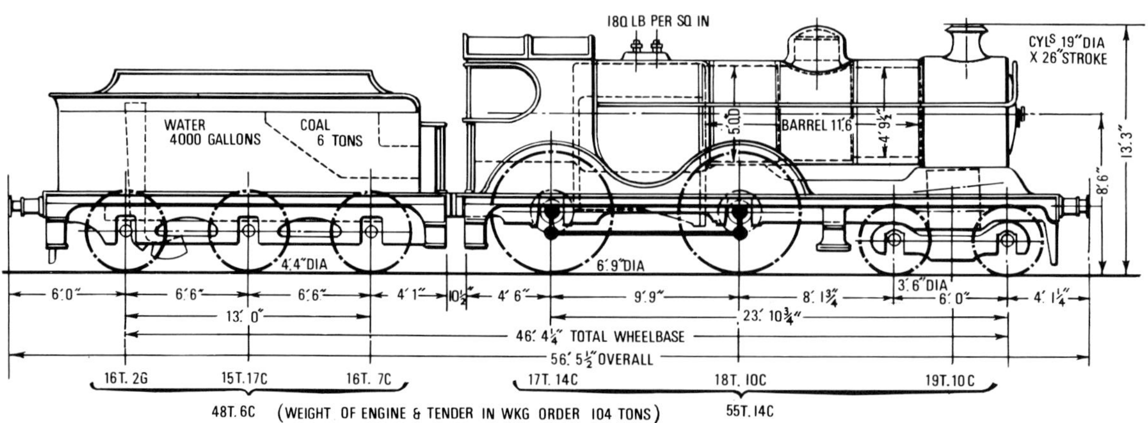

Left: In original GCR condition, Class 11B 4-4-0 No 113 heads an up slow near Willesden Green. Robinson's graceful chimney was particularly well proportioned on these engines. *Real Photographs*

Below: Also in original condition, Class 11B 4-4-0 No 1038 was photographed at Marylebone station awaiting departure with an up express. Gentlemen in straw boaters pause for the camera, having walked forward to inspect the engine. George Dow in his book *Great Central* says of Marylebone that it was '. . . graced by a cloistered calm which no other London terminal could rival'. It has not changed to this day! *LPC*

Above right: Robinson realised that a larger boiler would further improve the excellent capabilities of the '11B's, as loads got progressively heavier. Two were rebuilt to Class 11C in 1907, the new boiler being larger in diameter and having a longer firebox. The cabfront spectacles had to be altered and a shorter chimney was fitted, in this case with a capuchon lip. No 110 is seen in September 1910, while still nameless. Polished casing to four column safety valves. *V. R. Webster*

Centre right: The '11D' class was a further rebuild of the '11B', using the larger boiler of the '11C' but retaining the shorter firebox of the original type. Visually there was little to distinguish '11D' from '11C'; however the chimney lacked the capuchon lip seen in the previous picture of No 110, and there was no casing to the safety valves, as can be seen in this rear threequarter study of No 1027. *Ian Allan Library*

Below: Class D9 4-4-0 No 5112 (ex-GCR Class 11D No 112) seen in LNER condition with reduced height boiler mountings and vacuum relief valve behind the chimney. The GCR arrangement of safety valves has been replaced by a pair of Ross 'pop' safety valves. A tablet catcher has been fitted to the tender for working on the M&GN line. *Photomatic*

The LNER moved several of the class to the Great Easter Section where they remained for several years and some were drafted to the Midland & Great Northern in 1936, but otherwise they continued to operate in greatest number on the Cheshire Lines service, until the last was condemned in 1950.

Last of class withdrawn: 62305 (7/1950)
None preserved

Above: One wonders what J. G. Robinson's reactions would have been to the filthy state of his 4-4-0s in their final years. What a contrast this picture of No 62307 *Queen Mary* (ex-No 6021), at Trafford Park in June 1949, makes with the earlier pictures of the engines in GCR days! The nameplate is so encrusted with grime that it is scarcely visible on the leading splasher.
H. C. Casserley

Below: Most of the class ended their days on the CLC services, and here No 2325 (ex-No 6041) heads a lengthy Liverpool-Manchester express past Glazebrook in October 1946. The very squat dome cover fitted by the LNER is emphasised in this view, and the engine is attached to an older GCR tender, with plated coal rails.
H. C. Casserley

The basic dimensions of the engines were as follows:

	As built	'11C'	'11D' (Superheated)
Heating surface, tubes			
Large and small (sq ft):	1,248	1,478	1,119
Firebox (sq ft):	130	148	141
Total (evaporative) (sq ft):	1,378	1,626	1,260
Superheater (sq ft):	—	—	178
Superheater elements:	—	—	22
Combined heating surfaces (sq ft):	1,378	1,626	1,438
Grate area (sq ft):	21	26	21
Tractive effort (lbs at 85% BP):	17,730	17,730	17,730

GCR Class 8A, LNER Classes Q4 and Q1 (rebuild)*, BR Class 5F 0-8-0 Heavy Goods Engines
Introduced: 1902, 1942*
Total: 89, 13*

Together with the contemporary Class 8 4-6-0 locomotives this design heralded the beginning of the big engine policy on the GCR, and the two classes had much in common, with the cylinders, etc interchangeable and with closely similar boilers. Unlike the 4-6-0, the 0-8-0 was steadily increased in number between 1902 and 1911, when the design was modified into the famous Robinson, or ROD, 2-8-0. From their introduction the class proved to be the master of the of the tasks they were allotted, which included duties such as taking export coal from Yorkshire to Grimsby and Immingham, 55 laden wagons out and 80 empties back. Known as 'Old Ladies' to the GCR enginemen the 0-8-0 was not visually so well blended as others of Robinson's earlier classes, having outside cylinders which emphasised the heavy looking front end. These cylinders drove on to the third pair of wheels. While the leading and trailing splashers were separate, the former including a sandbox, those for the second and third coupled wheels were combined. Other features were typical of Robinson's earlier classes and

indeed they changed little over the years, apart from the fitting of superheated boilers to several, until the drastic alteration of a number to become tank engines was made to meet World War 2 needs.

The engines were built as follows (GCR numbers):

Nos 1052-4	Neilson, Reid	1902
Nos 56-9, 64/5/7/8, 70/1, 85-7, 91/2	Kitson	1903
Nos 135-40/2-53	Kitson	1904
Nos 1073-7	Kitson	1905
Nos 1132-44	Kitson	1909
Nos 39, 44/8/9, 62/3, 159-64, 212/3, 356, 401	Gorton	1909
Nos 956-65, 1174-9	Gorton	1910
Nos 1180-2	Gorton	1911

Fifteen of these engines were sent to France in 1917 for Railway Operating Division service, returning in 1919, but otherwise all remained on GCR lines and withdrawal started in 1934, reducing their number to 48 by the time the 1943 LNER scheme was prepared. By then four had been converted to 0-8-0T, so that the new numbers were 3200-43 and 9925-8.

The conversion to 0-8-0T already mentioned was a drastic rebuilding, but the original frames and cylinders were retained, although the drive for the valve gear was transferred from the third axle to the second. In order to make room at the rear for the cab and bunker the boiler barrel had to be shortened and this placed the firebox over the third axle, so raising the boiler in the frames. The side tanks, cabs and bunkers came from an order for LNER 'J50' class 0-6-0Ts which was cancelled after work had commenced. The original smokebox was retained, but a GNR pattern chimney was fitted. It was soon found that the water capacity was insufficient, so a second version was produced

Below: Class 8A outside-cylinder 0-8-0 heavy goods engine.

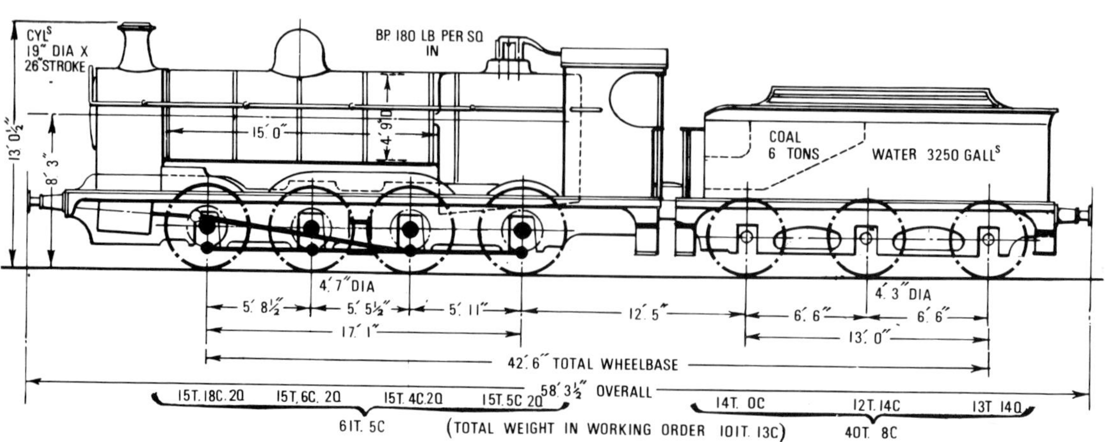

Above: In pre-Grouping days there was no clear preference for either inside or outside cylinders for eight-coupled goods engines, unlike the many 0-6-0 classes built over the years, which were almost universally inside-cylindered. Robinson chose to use two outside cylinders for his large goods engines, the '8A' class, no doubt influenced by a desire to standardise cylinders and motion with his contemporary Class 8 4-6-0. One of the 1903-04 Kitson-built examples of the large and rugged 0-8-0s is seen here; No 67. *LPC*

Below: Class 8A 0-8-0 No 1074 was one of the final batch of engines, built at Gorton in 1910-11, but it displays no noticeable change over the period of construction since 1902. Note the rerailing jack carried on the leading end of the running plate, and the open coal rails on the tender. The combined splasher over the centre pair of coupled wheels housed the sandbox. *LPC*

0531

Above: With a goods train load at Leicester, that seemingly stretches to infinity. Class 8A No 39 is illustrated; with tender with solid coal guards. The dirty condition of the engine, so untypical of GCR practice, suggests that this picture was taken during the 1914-18 war period when there was a shortage of cleaners. Note the whitewash on the three leading cattle trucks.
L&GRP courtesy David & Charles

Below: One of the superheated engines, LNER Class Q4/2 (GCR Class 8A) 0-8-0 No 3228 poses for the camera whilst on ballast train duties at Hougham in February 1949. Note the vacuum relief valve behind the inelegant chimney, and the reduced height of the dome. One engine of the class, No 184, was fitted with a side window cab and a No 6 standard boiler, with larger firebox, in 1923.   *C. C. B. Herbert*

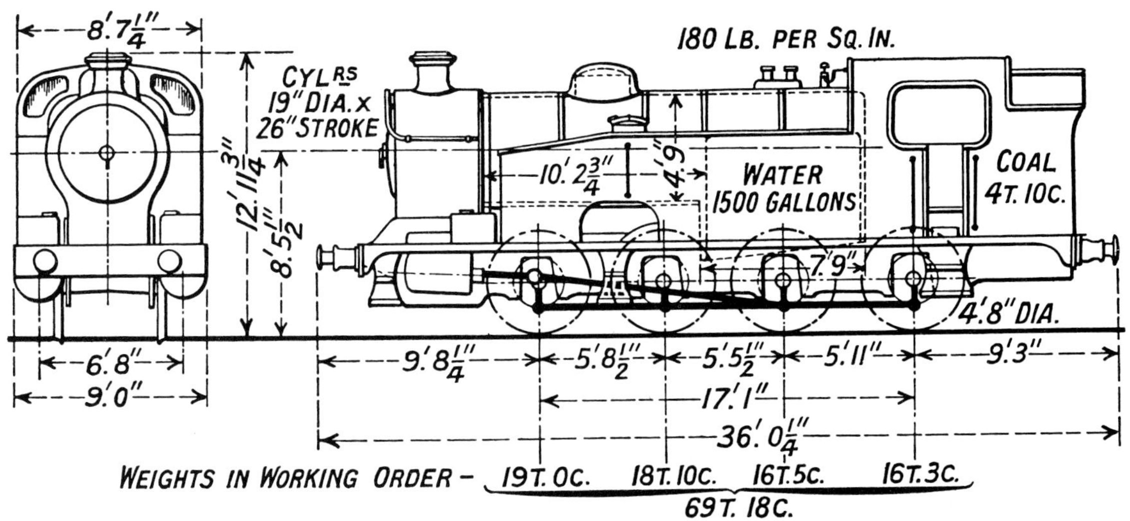

Top; LNER Class Q1/1 0-8-0T as first rebuilt from Class Q4 0-8-0, with hopper-type bunker. Class Q1/2 had an enlarged bunker with 500gal of water carried in a back tank.

Above: The official LNER view of the first conversion to Class Q1, No 5058 of 1942 finished in black wartime livery. Note the oval LNER plate on the bunkerside, this had a light blue background. The chimney design was pure Great Northern, as was the well rounded style of the cab roof. Hopper-type bunker fitted. *Ian Allan Library*

with the frames lengthened at the rear by 6in, so that a back tank containing 500gal could be fitted. These two versions were classified 'Q1/1' and 'Q1/2', with four and nine locomotives respectively.

In 1942 25 conversions were authorised, but only 13 were actually altered in 1942-5 as follows:

1942   5058, 5961, 5139 (9925-7)
1943   5048, 5070, 6077, (9928-30)
1944   5044, 5959, 5087, 5068 (9931-4)
1945   5147, 6179, 5138 (9935-7)

A further 22 conversions were authorised in 1945 but none of these took place; in fact this meant that it was planned to rebuild all the surviving engines; instead the unaltered engines were all scrapped by 1951. Of those altered two were sent to Scotland, working from Eastfield, two to the North Eastern area, initially at Gateshead and then Selby, while the remainder spent the greater part of their time at Sheffield, Immingham and Frodingham.

The postwar numbering of the engines was complicated, as follows: Nos 6053, 5071/86/91, 5135/9/40/3-5/8-51,   6073-5,   6137/8/41/4, 5049/62/3, 5212/3, 5356, 5401, 5956-8/60/3-5, 6174/8/81/2 were scrapped before the 1946 LNER renumbering scheme was drawn up; the remainder were allotted new numbers: 3200-3, 9925, 3204-27, 9927, 3228-30, 9928, 3231-7, 9926, 3238-43 respectively, but No 6175 did not become 3239 and Nos 5070, 6077, 5044, 5959, 5087, 5068, 5147, 6179 and 5138 became Nos 9929-37 as they were rebuilt after the scheme had been prepared in 1943.

Last of class withdrawn: '8A' 63204 (6/1951) 'Q1' 69936 (9/1959)
None preserved:

The basic dimensions of the class and of the 0-8-0T rebuilds were as follows:

	As built	Superheated	Rebuilt to 0-8-0T ('Q1')
Heating surface, tubes			
Large and small (sq ft):	1,625	1,198	1,068
Firebox (sq ft):	140	140	141
Total (evaporative) (sq ft):	1,665	1,338	1,209
Superheater (sq ft):	—	230	—
Superheater elements:	—	21	—
Combined heating surfaces (sq ft):	1,665	1,568	1,209
Grate area (sq ft):	23	$23\frac{1}{2}$	$23\frac{1}{2}$
Tractive effort (lbs at 85% BP):	25,645	31,325	25,644

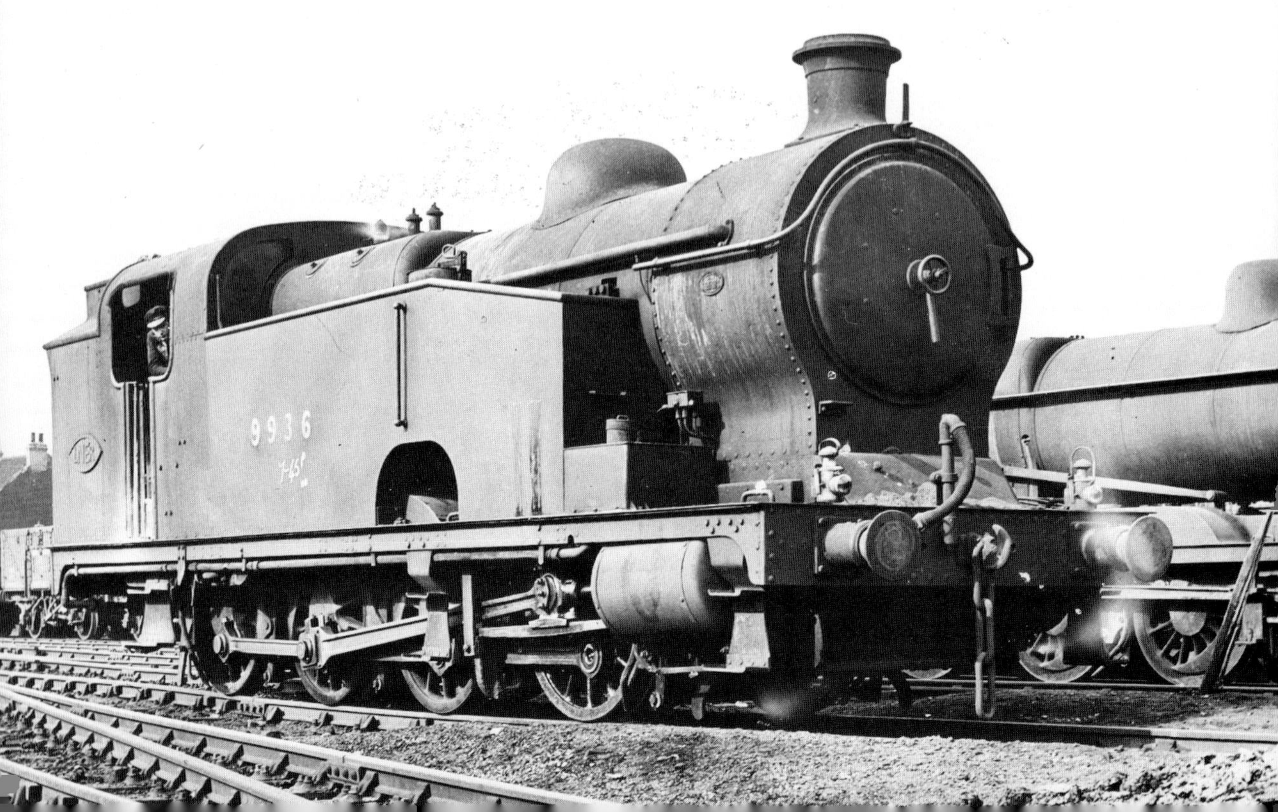

Below: Another view of a Class Q1/1, No 9936 (formerly No 6179) showing the small modified Gill Sans numerals at first used for the second 1946 renumbering scheme. *P. Ransome-Wallis*

GCR Class 8, LNER Class B5, BR Class 3MT
4-6-0 Express Goods Engines
Introduced: 1902
Total: 14

The first of Robinson's 4-6-0 classes was a good straightforward outside-cylinder type, with inside link motion, and this formed the basis of three other 4-6-0 classes, and the Atlantics. There were features in common with the Class 8A 0-8-0 and they remained virtually as built during their GCR days. Intended for fast fish trains from Grimsby to London they inevitably became known as the 'Fish' engines.

It was not until 1923 that any were superheated, when No 184 was fitted with a boiler of the type used on the '8K' 2-8-0. Another change to this engine made at the same time was the fitting of a side window cab. It was decided however to use the original size of boiler for superheating the class, but because of a deeper firebox, the replacement boiler had to be raised in the frames. The class was altered in 1926-36, No 184 reverting to its original size of boiler in 1927, and incidentally also losing the side window cab.

No 1072 was subjected to an unusual experimental device in 1912, when it received a Schleyder ash consumer. With this device ashes were drawn by vacuum from the bottom of the smokebox and fed into the firebox, so that in theory the unburnt fuel could be consumed!

When first built, tenders of 3,250gal capacity were fitted, but in 1906 the larger 4,000gal type was acquired in exchanges with other classes.

The two batches of this class were built as follows (GCR numbers):

Nos 1067-72	Neilson, Reid	1902
Nos 180-7	Beyer, Peacock	1904

Apart from No 6070 the initially allotted LNER 1946 numbers were 1300-12 and Nos 5186/7 became Nos 1311/2; however the new series was altered to Nos 1678-90, all being thus renumbered.

The 1902 batch of engines was shared between Neasden and Grimsby and many of the 1904 lot went to Gorton. As they were the largest engines on the GCR at the time it is not surprising that they were often used on expresses. The class was normally stationed on the northern part of the system and several finished their days on Cheshire Lines services.

Last of class withdrawn: 1686 (6/1950)
None preserved

The basic dimensions of the class were as follows:

	As built	Superheated
Heating surface, tubes		
Large and small (sq ft):	1,625	1,198
Firebox (sq ft):	130	140
Total (evaporative) (sq ft):	1,755	1,338
Superheater (sq ft):	—	230
Superheater elements:	—	21
Combined heating surfaces (sq ft):	1,755	1,568
Grate area (sq ft):	$23\frac{1}{2}$	$23\frac{1}{2}$
Tractive effort (lbs at 85% BP):	19,672	19,672

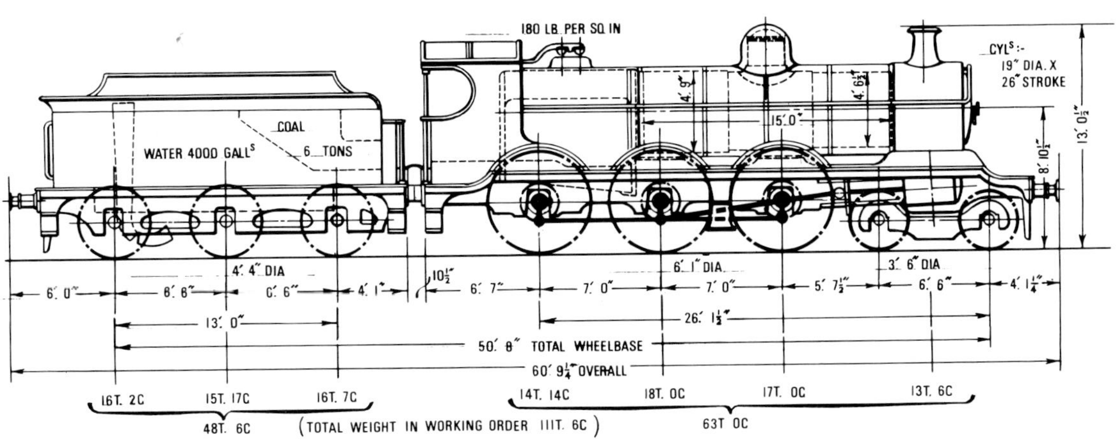

Below: Class 8 Express goods engine, as first introduced in 1902

Below: It is a pity that this photograph has suffered somewhat from the ravages of time, and that some of the detail of the engine has become lost. Nevertheless it is reproduced here because not only does it show a Class 8 4-6-0 'Fish engine', in immaculate original condition, but it also depicts the new bogie 15ton fish vans produced by the GCR for the traffic from Grimsby at the same time; 1902. This must have been the most modern goods train ensemble in Great Britain when photographed. The locomotive is No 1072, and has the original layout of two safety valve columns. *Ian Allan Library*

Bottom: A lovely study of one of the Beyer Peacock batch of 'Fish engines' No 181 of 1904, photographed on 13 May 1910. Four safety valve columns fitted, and rerailing jack carried on running plate at front end. *V. R. Webster*

Top: In LNER guise and black livery with red lining but still substantially in GCR form, Class B5 (ex-GCR Class 8) 4-6-0 No 6070 has a brass casing surrounding the four column safety valves and still proudly sports the Robinson chimney and dome.   *P. Ransome-Wallis*

Above: In LNER days the reduced height mountings of the superheated boiler, raised higher in the frames, with its poor chimney design, did nothing for the good looks of the 'Fish engines', as can be seen here in this broadside study of No 5183, with the fireman on the tender busily taking water from a shed column.   *Photomatic*

GCR Class 9K & 9L*, LNER Classes C13 & C14*, BR Class 2P
4-4-2T Passenger Tank Engines
Introduced: 1903, 1907*
Total: 52

Just as Robinson had developed an existing 2-4-2T into a 4-4-2T whilst on the WLWR, so he enlarged the design of the 1889-98 Parker and Pollitt 'double-enders' into a 4-4-2T, when further engines were needed for the expanding suburban traffic, especially in the London area. Although somewhat larger, these engines bore quite a strong resemblance to the Irish engines. Initially 20 were delivered in 1903, followed by another 20 in 1904-5, all of which became Class 9K. These were followed by another dozen in 1907 which were Class 9L. These differed principally in their coal and water capacity, as the bunker was narrowed at the top to improve rearward vision. Water pick-up gear was fitted to all 52, although not until after construction on the first 20, but this feature was later removed by the LNER. Only one of each class was superheated by the GCR, and then in 1926 the LNER commenced the more general fitting of superheaters, all being altered by 1935.

Below: Class 9K 4-4-2T design of 1903. The Class 9L version of 1907 carried 1,825gal of water and 4ton 6cwts of coal, and weighed 70ton 7cwts, in other respects the two types were very similar.

Right: Class 9K 4-4-2T No 47, seen standing in the rural calm of South Harrow station, circa 1907, working an up suburban train bunker first.

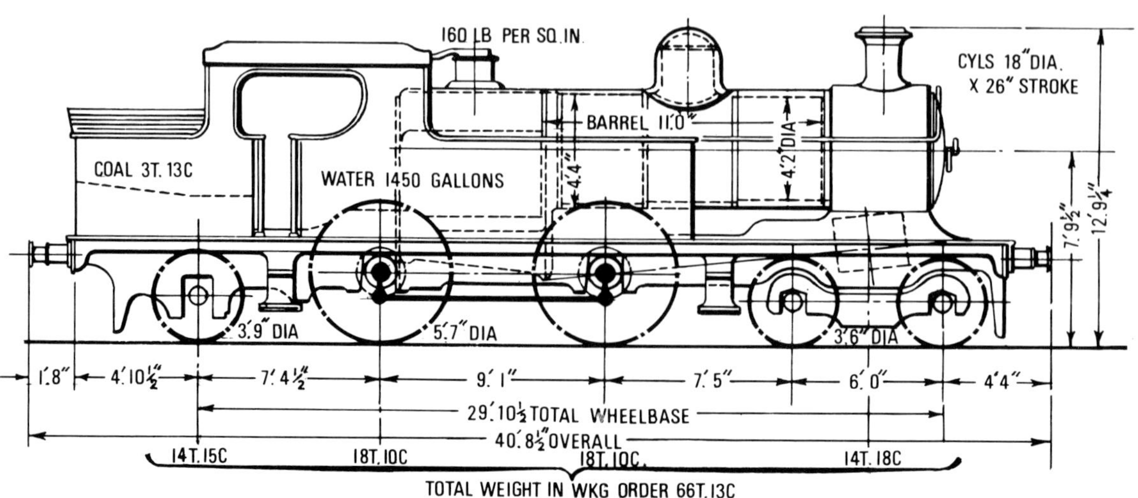

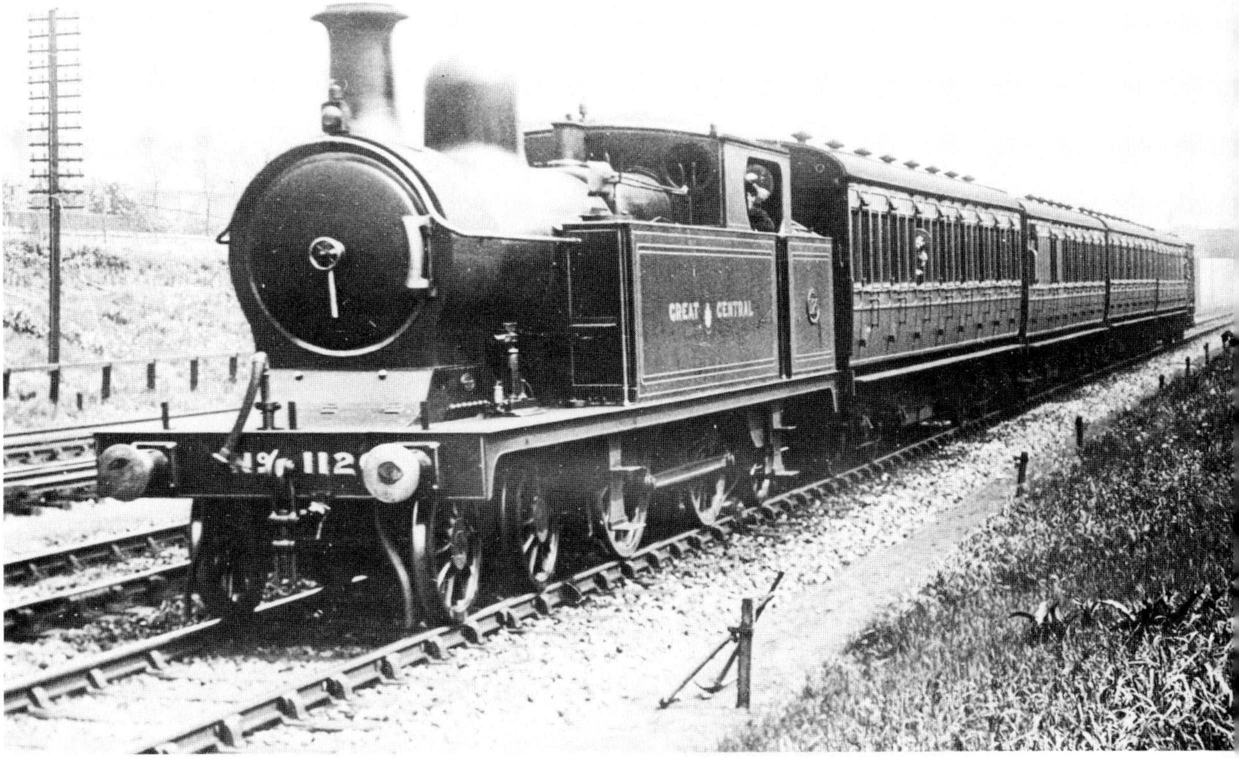

Above: A down local on the joint GC and Metropolitan lines, headed by Class 9L 4-4-2T No 1120, in original condition. These handsome tank engines displayed quite a resemblance to the engines of the same wheel arrangement that Robinson had produced for the WLWR   *H. Gordon Tidey*

Below: Class 9L 4-4-2T No 1120, showing the deeper and wider side tanks with increased capacity, and the inward sloping coal rails on the bunker. The cab roof was pitched slightly higher and a brass casing housed the safety valves. These engines went into service on the GW and GC Joint line.   *LPC*

Above right: Showing the distinctive inward slope of the bunker coal rails, designed to give better vision when running bunker first. This picture of Class 9L 4-4-2T No 1121 on a train near Denham, circa 1909, also shows the practice of painting the number on the back of the bunker. Note the two footsteps below the buffers.
H. Gordon Tidey

Centre right: Loss of the shapely Robinson chimney and its substitution with this ungainly affair did nothing for the looks of No 6131 of LNER Class C14 (GCR No 1131 of Class 9L). Note also the vacuum relief valve on the side of the smokebox. The engine still carries the casing for the safety valves. Photographed at Nottingham.
Photomatic

Below: An almost forgotten sight of steam days, once so familiar, is recalled here with the spectacle of Class C13 (ex-GCR Class 9K) No 67421 propelling an auto-train — or push-pull — from Oldham to Guide Bridge; near Parkbridge. The engine is fitted with vacuum control push-pull gear, and has for some reason, two vacuum relief valves on the smokebox, one behind the chimney and one alongside. Wooden coal guards added to the bunker sides. *J. Davenport*

The 52 locomotives of these two classes were built as follows (GCR numbers):

9K	Nos 1055-66	Vulcan Foundry	1903
9K	Nos 171/8/9/88/90/1/3/9	Gorton	1903
9K	Nos 2, 9, 18, 20/7-9, 47, 50-3	Gorton	1904
9K	Nos 457, 454-6, 310/57/9, 114/5, 453	Gorton	1905
9L	Nos 1120-31	Beyer, Peacock	1907

All were numbered in the LNER 1946 scheme, becoming Nos 7400-51 in the above order.

The majority of the '9K' and all of the '9L' engines went new to Neasden but after being displaced by the larger '9N' 4-6-2T of 1911, they became more scattered. Wrexham had some in 1905 and despite the severe gradients up from Connahs Quay they performed extraordinarily well, remaining in that area until after Nationalisation. In 1933 six of the Wrexham allocation were fitted with the GCR pattern mechanical control gear for pull and push trains. This control gear was heavy to operate, and required a lot of maintenance, so it was replaced in 1936-7 by LNER vacuum control equipment; two more were fitted in 1941, for working the Chesham branch trains. Most of the '9L' class were sent by the LNER to East Anglia, working from Ipswich and others performed well on former GNR lines in the West Riding. As the older 2-4-2T classes were withdrawn, so these engines replaced them in the Manchester area, where they became commonplace until withdrawal in 1957-60.

Last of class withdrawn: '9K' 67417 (1/1960)
'9L' 67450 (1/1960)
None Preserved

The basic dimensions were as follows:

	'9K'	*'9L'*	*'9K', '9L'*
	As built	*As built*	*Superheated*
Heating surface, tubes			
Large and small (sq ft):	955	955	785
Firebox (sq ft):	110	105	108
Total (evaporative) (sq ft):	1,065	1,060	893
Superheater (sq ft):	—	—	138
Superheater elements:	—	—	18
Combined heating surfaces (sq ft):	1,065	1,060	1,031
Grate area (sq ft):	20	19½	19½
Tractive effort (lbs at 85% BP):	17,100	17,100	17,100

Below: A lovely portrayal of a Robinson Class 9K 4-4-2T in BR days as No 67439, with the sunlight casting a dramatic moving shadow upon the lineside as the exhaust wafts from the chimney and dusts the carriages of the Manchester (London Road)-Hayfield stopping train it is seen hauling near Romiley in July 1951. One of the more attractive features of the engines, which they retained throughout their lives, was the distinctive shape of the cab roof. *T. Lewis*

GCR Class 8B & 8C*, LNER Class C4 & B1* (later B18)
4-4-2 & 4-6-0* Express Passenger Engines
Introduced: 1903
Totals: 27, 2*

Robinson's first large express locomotives were built by Beyer, Peacock, to designs actually prepared by that firm, and the initial order consisted of four engines delivered in 1903-4 as follows:

4-4-2 '8B' Nos 192 and 194
4-6-0 '8C' Nos 195 and 196

The two types were identical in virtually all respects and the idea was to compare the merits of four- and six-coupled engines for express work, it being possible if necessary to convert the Atlantics to 4-6-0. Unlike Churchward on the GWR who did the same thing at the time with his 'Star' class, Robinson found that the Atlantics were quite satisfactory for the weight of trains then running, and so they were multiplied. To make the two classes compatible in the first place, the firebox was not as deep as it could have been on the Atlantics, but when more were built advantage was taken of the lack of the trailing coupled wheels to deepen the firebox and increase its heating surface.

These graceful engines were considered by many to be Robinson's most handsome design, particularly the Atlantic version, which the enginemen dubbed 'Jersey Lilies' after the famed singer of the time, Lily Langtry. These engines handled the hardest jobs to and from Marylebone, and when the practice developed of changing engines at Leicester, the Atlantics were associated in quantity with that shed for 30 years. Both the 4-6-0 engines, however, remained at Neasden, after an initial spell at Gorton.

It seems that Robinson felt the need to try out a three-cylinder simple engine, so No 1090 was converted in 1908. This engine had divided drive, with the inside-cylinder driving the leading coupled axle and three sets of Walschaerts valve gear, having the expansion links in line. The outside valve gear fitted rather detracted from the appearance of the engine. Classified 8J No 1090 reverted to standard in 1922.

The fitting of superheaters was started in 1912, but it was not until 1936 that the job was completed. Similarly the fitting of new cylinders with piston valves took place over many years and this was not always coincident with superheating; seven engines were never altered. Both the 4-6-0 engines were superheated, and fitted with new piston valve cylinders, in 1912 and 1927 respectively (although No 195 again ran with a saturated boiler in 1920-6).

The first four engines of 1903-4 had 3,250gal tenders with water pick-up when new, but before long they acquired the larger tenders. The remainder of the Atlantics always had the 4,000gal tenders.

Below: Class 8B 4-4-2 Express Passenger Engine No 192 (with 19½in by 26in cylinder diameter) as first delivered in 1903. On the second batch of 4-4-2 engines and subsequent orders the firebox was deeper.

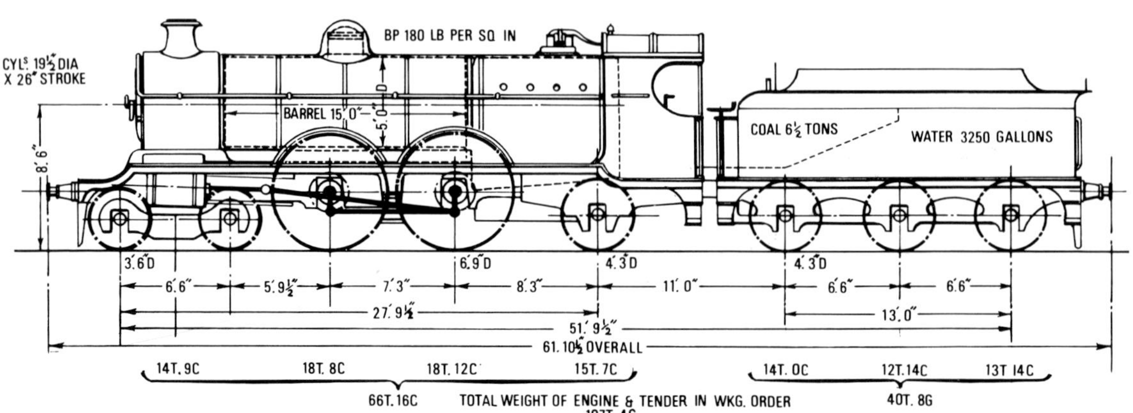

Above: The typical flowing curves of Robinson's engines are well seen in this view of the second of the 4-6-0s, built by Beyer Peacock, No 196 of Class 8C. The GCR coat of arms was carried on the centre splasher and a monogram on the other two. Robinson evidently found that the 4-4-2 version of the design suited GCR needs, and no further 4-6-0s of Class 8C were ordered, although he went on to produce the smaller wheeled Class 8F version for express goods work, in 1906 (see Section 9.) *LPC*

Below: Comparison with the preceding picture shows just how close the 4-6-0s and 4-4-2s were in their overall design. Indeed the Atlantics could have been converted to 4-6-0s with relative ease, had Robinson so decided. This picture of Class 8B No 1085, one of the North British-built batch of 1905, serves also to show the later standard Robinson tender design with solid plates as coal guards, whereas the initial four engines of Class 8B and 8C had tenders with coal rails. The NBL-built batch had an increased working pressure of 200lb/sq in. *S. W. A. Newton*

Above left: A classic study of a 'Jersey Lily', with a down Manchester train near Wembley. The engine is another of the NBL-built batch, No 1086, of 1905. In the proceding year the GCR had used engines of this class on through excursion workings over GWR metals as far as Plymouth, Weymouth and Weston-super-Mare. In October 1904 No 267 worked through from Manchester to Plymouth (374 miles) with the same crew throughout, In the following year Nos 265/287 also reached Plymouth, but after that Bristol was the furthest point reached.
Ian Allan Library

Below left: Another view of Class 8C 4-6-0 No 196, in truly immaculate condition with all the unpainted metal surfaces brightly burnished. The location is Leicester on 20 July 1910 and the engine is standing at the head of the 12.15 London-Manchester train. The leading van went through to Grimsby, hence this train was sometimes called the 'Grimsby Boat Express'. What a typical scene of the classic days of steam this picture presents, with the four column safety valves gently blowing whilst the fireman is in the tender pulling the coal forward and the driver is on the running plate tending the engine with an oil can. *W. Bradshaw*

Above: One of the Class 8B simple two-cylinder Atlantics, No 1090, was selected by Robinson for conversion to a three-cylinder engine, in 1908. This became the only engine of Class 8J, and had Walschaerts valve gear with cylinders of 16in by 26in. It ran in this condition until 1922. Note the footsteps added to the front end, ahead of the leading bogie wheel, because the outside Walschaerts motion required the removal of the large footsteps located between the two coupled wheels. *Ian Allan Library*

Below: Class 8B 4-4-2 No 1090 after return to its original two-cylinder condition, in 1922. Note the altered shape of the dome cover, and the two Ross 'pop' safety valves in place of the originals. Note that the leading footsteps have been removed but the original large central footsteps have not been replaced.
L&GRP courtesy David & Charles

Above: Apart from the excursion train wanderings already mentioned, one 'Jersey Lily' visited a number of places in 1925, when used by the Bridge Testing Committee. The class was selected because of its heavy hammerblow effect upon the track. The engine, LNER No 5360, was worked specially over bridges and viaducts at Lancaster; Runcorn; several places on LNER lines; Somerton, Langport and Stoke Cannon on the GWR and Poole on the Southern. In this picture No 5360 stands at Blaby in October 1925, ready for testing a bridge near Narborough. In the background is another test engine, ex-LYR 0-8-0 No 1456.   *E. G. Shoults*

The engines of these two classes were built at follows (GCR numbers):

8B 4-4-2	Nos 192/4	Beyer, Peacock	1903
8C 4-6-0	No 195	Beyer, Peacock	1903
8C 4-6-0	No 196	Beyer, Peacock	1904
8B 4-4-2	Nos 263-7	Beyer, Peacock	1904
8B 4-4-2	Nos 1083-94	North British	1905
8B 4-4-2	Nos 260-2, 358/60-3	Gorton	1906

The Atlantics were allotted new 1946 LNER numbers 2900-25 in the above order, apart from No 6090 already withdrawn; Nos 5266 and 6087 were not actually renumbered. The 4-6-0 engines were to have become Nos 1470/1, but actually were renumbered 1479/80.

It was not until the arrival of the LNER 'B17' ('Sandringham') class on the GCR section in 1936 that dispersal in numbers began to sheds away from the GCR main line. Some were sent to work Kings Cross to Cambridge trains, but they all eventually congregated in Lincolnshire. The two 4-6-0 engines had a more nomadic life, spending time at Woodford, Leicester and Colwich.

Last of class withdrawn: '8B' 2918 (2/1950)
'8C' 1480 (12/1947)
None preserved

The basic dimensions of the initial series of two-cylinder simple 4-4-2s/4-6-0s were as follows:

	As built	Superheated
Heating surface, tubes		
Large and small (sq ft):	1,778	1,349
Firebox (sq ft):	133	133
Total (evaporative) (sq ft):	1,911	1,482
Superheater (sq ft):	—	242
Superheater elements:	—	22
Combined heating surfaces (sq ft):	1,911	1,724
Grate area (sq ft):	$26\frac{1}{4}$	$26\frac{1}{4}$
Tractive effort (lbs at 85% BP)	17,729†	21,658*

† 19in diameter cylinders
* 21in diameter cylinders
Notes (a) When new Nos 192/5 had $19\frac{1}{2}$in by 26in cylinders and Nos 194/6 had 19in by 26in cylinders
(b) Later batches of 4-4-2s had a deeper firebox with an area of 153sq ft, giving an evaporative total of 1,931 sq ft.

Above left: In LNER apple green passenger livery as No 5196 of Class B1 (later B18), the second of the two 4-6-0s had by this time received a superheated boiler. Comparison with the picture of it as GCR No 196 on pages 49/50 shows little change except the revised chimney and dome design, twin Ross 'pop' safety valves, and removal of footsteps between leading and centre coupled wheels. Vacuum relief valve behind chimney. Photographed at Woodford in 1933. *Photomatic*

Centre left: The artless chimney and squat dome of LNER days, and the black livery, still could not demean the grand style of Robinson's classic Atlantic, as this photograph of No 6089 amply demonstrates.

Below: Every inch a thoroughbred, despite the altered chimney shape and the removal of the large footsteps between the coupled wheels, LNER Class C4 4-4-2 (ex-GCR Class 8B) No 5192, one of the original pair of 'Jersey Lilies' leans to a curve with an express in prewar days. *P. Rowledge collection*

GCR Class 8D & 8E*, LNER Class C5
4-4-2 Express Passenger Engines
Introduced: 1905, 1906*
Total: 4
'The Compounds'

Although these engines were outwardly identical, there were sufficient differences in the layout of the frames for the GCR to regard each pair as separate classes. The LNER however later put them all in the one class as their 'C5'. A very marginal coal economy of $2-2\frac{1}{2}$lb/mile was claimed for these compound engines compared with the 'simple' Atlantics. Although, in 1908, Robinson said that he was inclined to build more compounds, he did not enlarge the class; in fact the reverse could have happened as they were designed for easy conversion to 'simples'. As on so many other railways it was the introduction of superheating that demonstrated in practical terms that compounding was an over-rated benefit.

The compound arrangement was such that the high pressure cylinder was inside the frames and drove the leading coupled axle, and this had a 10in diameter piston valve, sited beneath the cylinder and inclined downwards to the front in order to maintain some directness of drive. The two low pressure outside cylinders had slide valves; each valve was driven by independent link motion and the cranks were set so that the low pressure were at 90° to each other, the high pressure at 270° to each of them so that there were four beats per wheel revolution. Apart from the application of superheating, in 1911-27, the engines were never radically altered throughout their working lives.

The four compounds were built as follows (GCR numbers):

8D	No 258	Gorton	1905
8D	No 259	Gorton	1906
8E	Nos 364/5	Gorton	1906

In the 1946 renumbering scheme they became Nos 2895-8 in the above order.

The names of the four engines were respectively those of the senior director of the company, the reigning monarch, the wife of the chairman of the company (being renamed when he came a lord) and a former general manager.

Until 1920-1 all four worked from Gorton. They did not usually work so far afield as the '8B' Atlantics, but No 258 got to Bristol in 1907, and then in 1908 to Stratford-upon-Avon via the SMJR from Woodford. There were three occasions when they were chosen to work Royal trains, in the period 1907-12. From Gorton all four went to Leicester, then in 1932-3 they were moved to Immingham, where they spent the rest of their time. In the Lincolnshire area they normally worked to Sheffield or on the Cleethorpes to New Holland service.

Last of class withdrawn: '8D' 2896 (4/1947); '8E' 2897 (12/1947)
None preserved

The basic dimensions of the compound 4-4-2s were as follows:

	As built	Superheated
Heating surface, tubes:		
Large and small (sq ft):	1,778	1,349
Firebox (sq ft):	153	154
Total (evaporative) (sq ft):	1,931	1,503
Superheater (sq ft):	—	242
Superheater elements:	—	22
Combined heating surfaces (sq ft):	1,931	1,745
Grate area (sq ft):	$26\frac{1}{4}$	$26\frac{1}{4}$
Tractive effort (lbs at 85% BP):	21,658	21,658

* No general arrangement drawing of Class 8D/8E is reproduced, as it was basically similar to Class 8B, reproduced in Section 7.

Top right: Class 8D Compound 4-4-2 No 258 *The Rt Hon Viscount Cross, GCB, GCSI;* first of the four compounds to be delivered, is seen here at Leicester Central on 15 July 1910, with the driver attending to the motion, from the running plate, and with the inspection covers below the smokebox on the front end open. Viscount Cross was one of the GCR directors. *V. R. Webster*

Centre right: The superb proportions of Robinson's Atlantics were apparent from whichever angle they were viewed. This broadside of Class 8E No 364 *Lady Henderson* shows just how well balanced but bold these massive engines were. The four compounds all carried names, with the nameplate on the trailing splasher with the GCR monogram below. The leading splasher carried the coat-of-arms, which was repeated on the tender sides. *Real Photographs*

Right: Taking water on the troughs near Charwelton in 1929, LNER Class C5 No 5364 *Lady Faringdon* (ex-GCR No 364 *Lady Henderson)* is seen at the head of an up Sheffield express. Plain LNER style chimney and vacuum relief valve added to side of smokebox. *Real Photographs*

GREAT CENTRAL

364
GREAT CENTRAL

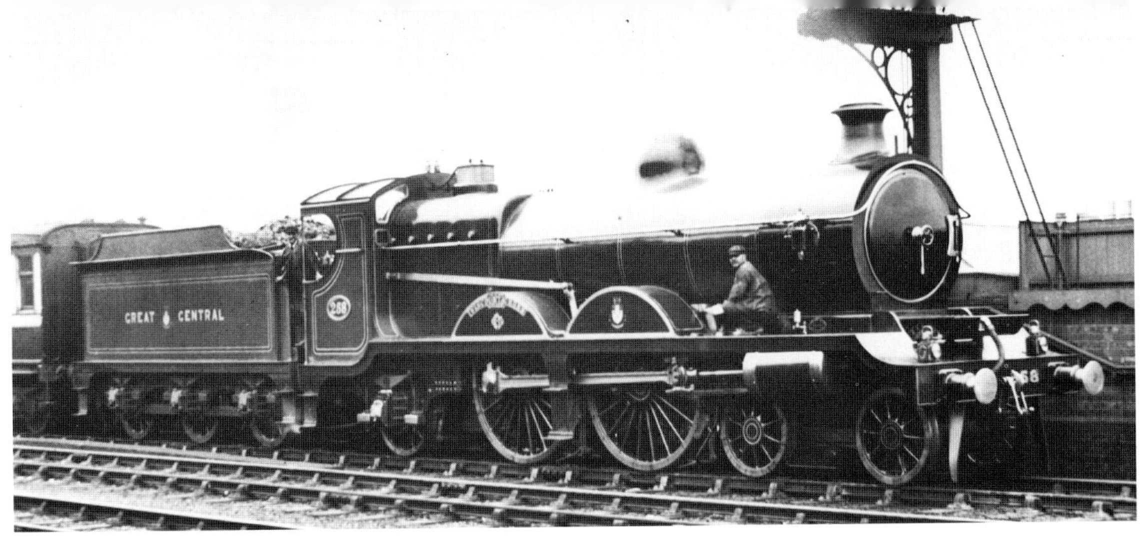

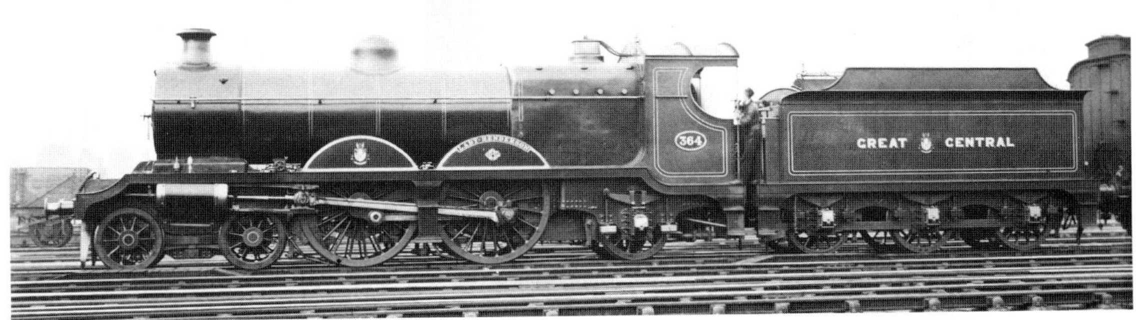

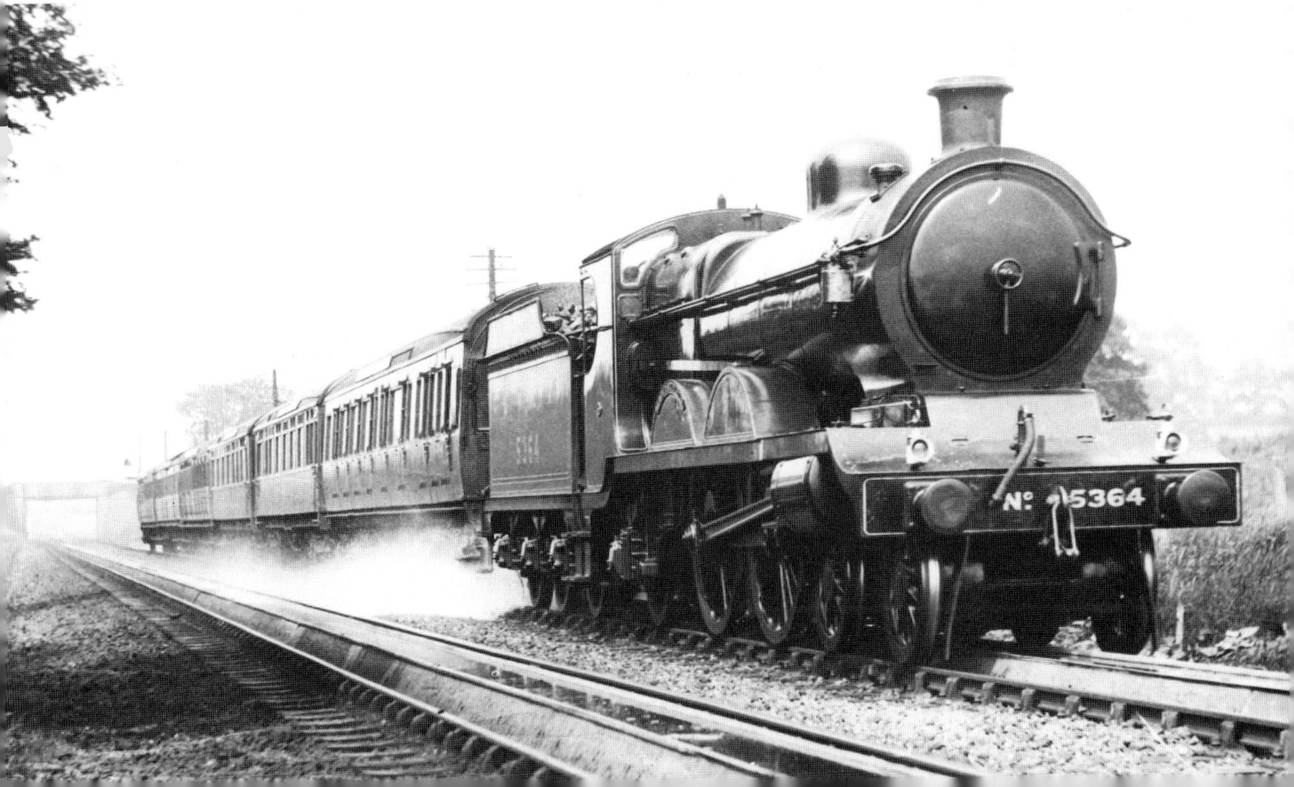
Nº 5364

GCR Class 8F, LNER Class B4, BR Class 4P
4-6-0 Express Goods Engines
Introduced: 1906
Total: 10 'Immingham'

These engines were a copy of the '8C' 4-6-0 Nos 195 and 196 and they differed only in having smaller coupled wheels, reduced by 3in. They were designed for fast goods and fish traffic but they were actually used more on passenger work. When still quite new No 1097 worked a special to the ceremony of cutting the first sod at Immingham docks, and thus acquired the name *Immingham*, which also gave to the class its popular name.

The engines were built as follows (GCR numbers):

Nos 1095-1104   Beyer, Peacock   1906

The numbers allotted initially in the LNER renumbering scheme were 1490-9; No 6095 was withdrawn unaltered and the remainder actually became Nos 1481-9 in the above order.

None were superheated by the GCR, but all were so altered by the LNER in 1925-8, with six also getting new cylinders with piston valves. The GCR green was the class colour for only a short while when new, and for a long time they were in black livery but No 6097 *Immingham* re-appeared in the apple green in the short-lived postwar shceme. All the others remained black.

The class was at first shared among Neasden,

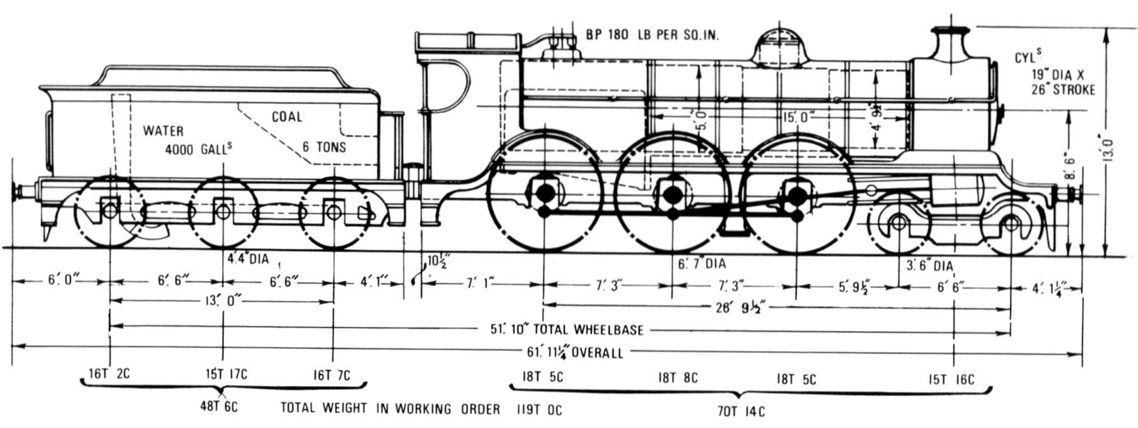

Left: A striking shot of Class 8F No 1100 (with casing added to the safety valves) at the head of a mixed train, with vans at the rear. *L&GRP courtesy David & Charles*

Below left: Class 8F ('Immingham') 4-6-0.

Above: Class 8F 4-6-0 No 1098, as built by Beyer Peacock at Gorton in 1906. This smaller wheeled two-cylinder design quickly found its way on to passenger work as well as the express goods and fish traffic for which it was primarily intended. Four column safety valve without casing. *LPC*

Gorton and Immingham, but when more powerful engines became available, they were concentrated in the northern part of the GCR. Some were moved by the LNER for a short spell on to the GN/GE joint line between Doncaster and March, and then in 1925 they were all sent to former GNR lines in the West Riding, then becoming regular visitors to Kings Cross and the east coast resorts. About 10 years later some were moved to Lincolnshire depots, and *Immingham* had the distinction of being the last GCR 4-6-0 to work on the London extension. This was in July 1949 when it travelled as far south as Banbury. This engine was also the last GCR 4-6-0 to remain in service.

Last of class withdrawn: 1482 11/1950.
None preserved

The basic dimensions of the class were as follows:

	As built	Superheated
Heating surfaces, tubes:		
Large and small (sq ft):	1,818	1,349
Firebox (sq ft):	133	133
Total (evaporative) (sq ft):	1,951	1,482
Superheater (sq ft):	—	242
Superheater elements:	—	22
Combined heating surfaces (sq ft):	1,951	1,724
Grate area (sq ft):	$26\frac{1}{4}$	$26\frac{1}{4}$
Tractive effort (lbs at 85% BP):	18,178	22,206*

* With 21in diameter cylinders

Right: With reduced height boiler mountings, ugly chimney and two Ross 'pop' safety valves, No 6103 of LNER Class B4 (ex-GCR Class 8F No 1103), is illustrated. At least the LNER granted the engines fully lined green livery, whereas in later GCR days they had been in the lined black. Vacuum relief valve behind chimney, and large footsteps removed from between leading and centre coupled wheels. *Real Photographs*

Centre right: The provision of a more shapely chimney, within the restrictions of the LNER loading gauge (note also the flattened top of the dome cover) certainly restored something of the former style to the class. No 6104 (ex-GCR No 1104, and last one built) was photographed at Escrick, between Selby and York, with a Newcastle-Harwich train in August 1938. Glass sightscreen added to cabside on drivers' side. *E. R. Wethersett*

Below right: Also showing the folding glass sightscreen added to the cabsides by the LNER (a feature which was intended to give added protection to the enginemen when looking out of the cabsides at speed), Class B4 No 1489 is seen here shortly before withdrawal, near Pyewipe Junction, Lincoln on 19 April, 1947. By this time the Class were past their prime and only four engines survived into BR ownership. These were No 61482/3/5/8. No 1489 is illustrated in plain black wartime livery, but some of the engines received postwar apple green, including *Immingham*, which was withdrawn in 1950 as last of the class. Note the coal rail tender (with plates added behind), from an earlier GCR locomotive. *H. C. Casserley*

GCR Class 8G, LNER Class B9, BR Class 5MT
4-6-0 Mixed-Traffic Engines
Introduced: 1906
Total: 10

The 10 engines of this class followed immediately after the '8F' class and were generally similar, except that they had 5ft 3in diameter coupled wheels, instead of 6ft 6in. The boiler was a hybrid, having the barrel of the Atlantics, and the smaller firebox of the '8' class 4-6-0 engines. In 1910 No 1109 was fitted with a smaller boiler of the type used on the '8' class, but in 1919 it reverted to standard. Superheating of the class was begun in 1924, using the boiler fitted to the '8A' class, and all were altered by 1929; the boiler centre line was raised because of the deeper firebox. Only one, No 6109, received new cylinders with piston valves, and although the performance of this engine was improved measurably, no others were altered.

The engines were built as follows (GCR numbers):

Nos 1105-14   Beyer, Peacock   1906

The 1946 renumbering scheme numbers initially allotted were 1342-51, but they actually became Nos 1469-78 in the above order.

The class was mostly associated with Gorton until the end of World War 2, although a few had been stationed at Lincoln until early LNER days. All finished their days at Cheshire Lines sheds, where they were not normally involved in passenger work.

Last of class withdrawn: 1475 (5/1949)
None preserved.

The basic dimensions of the class were as follows:

	As built	Superheated
Heating surface, tubes:		
Large and small (sq ft):	1,818	1,198
Firebox (sq ft):	133	140
Total (evaporative) (sq ft):	1,951	1,338
Superheater (sq ft):	—	230
Superheater elements:	—	21
Combined heating surfaces (sq ft):	1,951	1,568
Grate area (sq ft):	26	$23\frac{1}{2}$
Tractive effort (lbs at 85% BP):	22,438	22,438

Left: The smaller wheels of the Class 8G 4-6-0 necessitated a dip in the running plate behind the cylinders in order to retain the decorum of splashers! The GCR livery for these engines was the goods black with red and white lining. No 1113 is illustrated when new, in this livery. *A. B. MacLeod collection*

Below: Class 8G two-cylinder 4-6-0 mixed-traffic design of 1906.

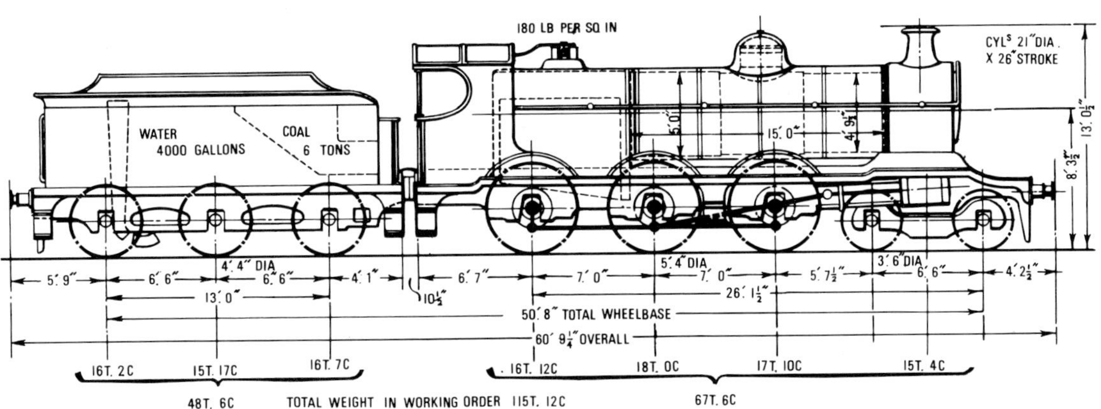

GREAT CENTRAL

Above: Evidence of the enginemen's pride can be seen in the burnished motif on the smokebox door, and in the general sparkle of Class 8G No 1114; complete with two rerailing jacks on the front end. The train is an August 1910 troop special, with horses travelling in the whitewashed vans behind the leading brakevan, from which members of HM forces are leaning to gain air on what was a very hot day, to judge from the haze in the left background.   *V. R. Webster*

Above far left: An interesting and later picture of a Class 8G in black GCR livery is this one of No 1110, carrying a GCR style brass numberplate with the new LNER number 6110, but otherwise not altered to show its new ownership. Apart from the addition of a brass casing to the four column safety valves the engine has not been altered, but it has lost its original tender for an earlier Robinson tender with open coal rails.
Lens of Sutton

Left: Somehow the squat boiler mountings of LNER days quite suited these small-wheeled 4-6-0s; being more in proportion with the rest of the engine. Despite the plain black postwar livery of Class B9 No 1470 in this picture, someone has made the effort to polish the brass beading to the splashers. Vacuum relief valve behind later style chimney, and Ross 'pop' safety valves fitted.
Ian Allan Library

The engines were built as follows (GCR numbers):

Nos 60/1, 89, 157, 324, 538	Gorton	1906
No 277	Gorton	1914

The seven engines became Nos 8204-10 in the above order in the LNER 1946 renumbering scheme.

GCR Class 5A, LNER Class J63, BR Class 0F
0-6-0T Shunting Engines
Introduced: 1906
Total: 7

When various small tank engines were in need of replacement, Robinson produced an up to date version of Pollitt's Class 5 0-6-0ST design of 1897. The same frames, cylinders, wheels, motion and boiler were used, but the new class had side tanks instead of a saddletank, and these had a greater water capacity; a larger cab was fitted. Quite smart in appearance, the first two, Nos 60 and 61, were fitted with condensing gear and sent to Liverpool, where one worked as the pilot at the Central Station (which had a tunnel immediately at the platform end), but later, non-condensing engines performed the job. Liverpool had some engines of this class until 1935-6, but the majority worked at Immingham. Odd examples were to be found at Wrexham and Bidston at times. The most interesting transfer was that of No 538 to St Margarets (Edinburgh) for a short while in 1935, being used at Granton.

The seven engines lasted well into British Railways days, being displaced by diesel shunters in 1955-7.

The basic dimensions of the class were as follows:

Heating surface, tubes
Large and small (sq ft):	530
Firebox (sq ft):	60
Total (evaporative) (sq ft):	590
Grate area (sq ft):	60
Tractive effort (lbs at 85% BP):	10,260

Below: Class 5A 0-6-0T design, introduced 1906.

Above right: Class 5A 0-6-0T No 538, last of the Gorton batch of 1906. When first delivered the first engine of the class, No 60 had a large Robinson-style chimney; somewhat oversize for such a diminutive locomotive. The revised chimney design as seen here, was a much smaller affair. Nos 60/61 had condensing gear fitted and a warning bell prominently mounted on the cab roof, for use in the Liverpool dock area. Note cabfront spectacle in open position. *LPC*

Below right: LNER Class J63 0-6-0T No 68207 (in BR days), originally GCR No 157, and not much altered in appearance since building; photographed at Immingham. The warning bell was later placed on the motion bracket of those engines carrying one, and driven by the valve gear. *D. Penney*

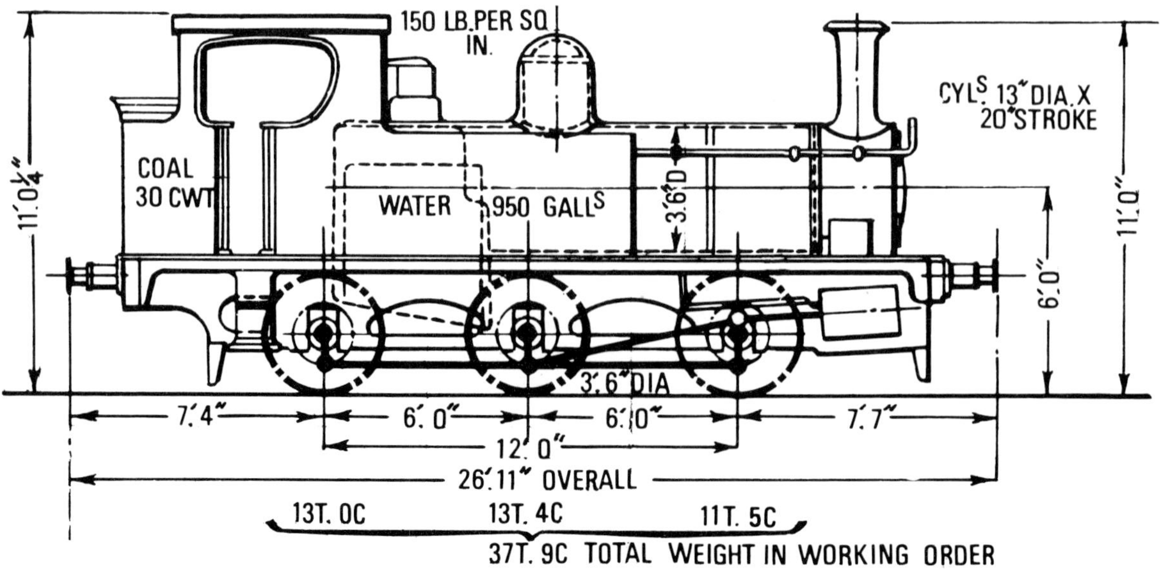

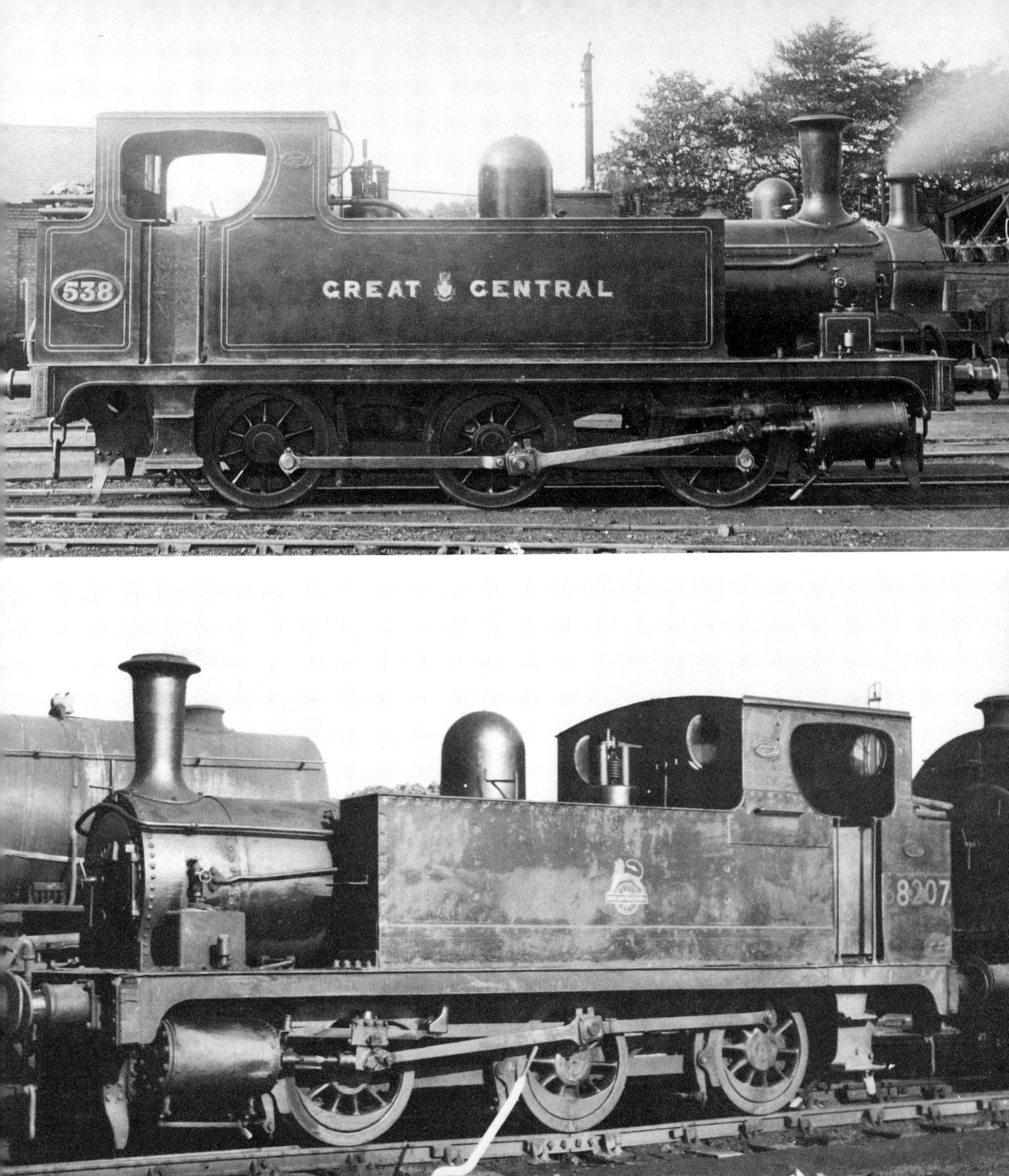

GCR Class 8H, LNER Class S1, BR Class 7F
0-8-4T Hump Shunting Engines
Introduced: 1907
Total: 6

Greatly enhanced engine power was needed when the GCR opened their massive new hump yard at Wath, near Mexborough. Until then the GCR had relied on moderately sized 0-6-2T and somewhat smaller 0-6-0ST for such work, but the new yard was beyond their powers. So a tank version of Class 8A was built, although some parts standard with other classes were also used. There were three cylinders, the outside pair driving the third coupled axle, and the inside driving the second, with link motion and direct drive to the valves of the former, and indirect drive through a rocking shaft to the latter. A bigger boiler was used, being similar to those built for the Atlantics and '8C' and '8F' 4-6-0 engines. A novelty, so far as the GCR was concerned was the use of a power reverser.

Even these massive engines had difficulty in hump-shunting during poor weather, and sometimes had to be used in pairs! In LNER days Gresley decided that this was a good case for providing a booster, so No 6171 was fitted with a new bogie in 1931; the bogie wheels were of smaller diameter than the old bogie and the steam powered booster was reversible, although in practice it was found not to be of any value in back gear, so that feature remained unused.

When the LNER developed Whitemoor, near March on the GE section, as the principal yard for East Anglia No 6170 was sent for trials in 1931, and as a result two more, LNER Nos 2798 and 2799 (booster fitted) were constructed in 1932, the last new engines built to Robinson's designs. These displaced Nos 6172 and 6173 at Wath, so that the latter could be used at March. The new engines were built at Gorton, although originally it was planned to build them at Doncaster, and they had superheater boilers, larger bunkers, reduced water capacity and side window cabs. The former GCR engines were fitted with superheater boilers in

Below: The drawing depicts the later, booster-fitted LNER Class S1 version of the GCR Class 8H 0-8-4T; with side window cab. Boiler pressure was later increased to 200lb/sq in.

Right: A classic study of a hump-shunter actually poised on the hump, and demonstrating the flexibility of the springs on the coupled wheels and bogie. LNER Class S1 No 6173 (ex-GCR Class 8H No 1173, built in 1908) has changed but little since building, except for the ugly chimney, squat dome and twin Ross 'pop' safety valves. *P. Ransome-Wallis*

Below right' The original form of the Class 8H 0-8-4Ts is well illustrated in this official picture of No 1171 in workshop grey livery, as built by Beyer Peacock in 1907. Note the power reverser located under the boiler inside the frames, and the bogie brakes. The first engines were built specifically for the Wath yard, near Mexborough. When new they were the most powerful locomotives in Great Britain. *Ian Allan Library*

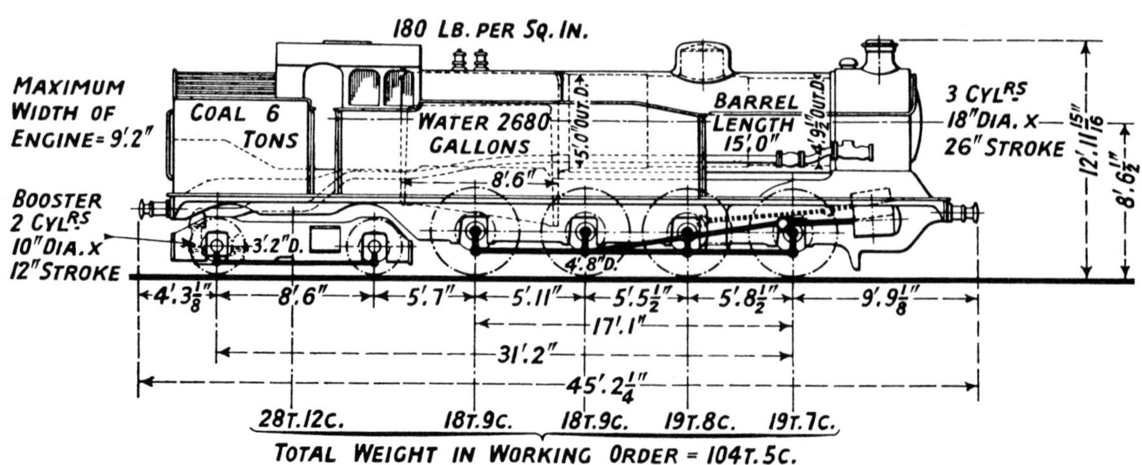

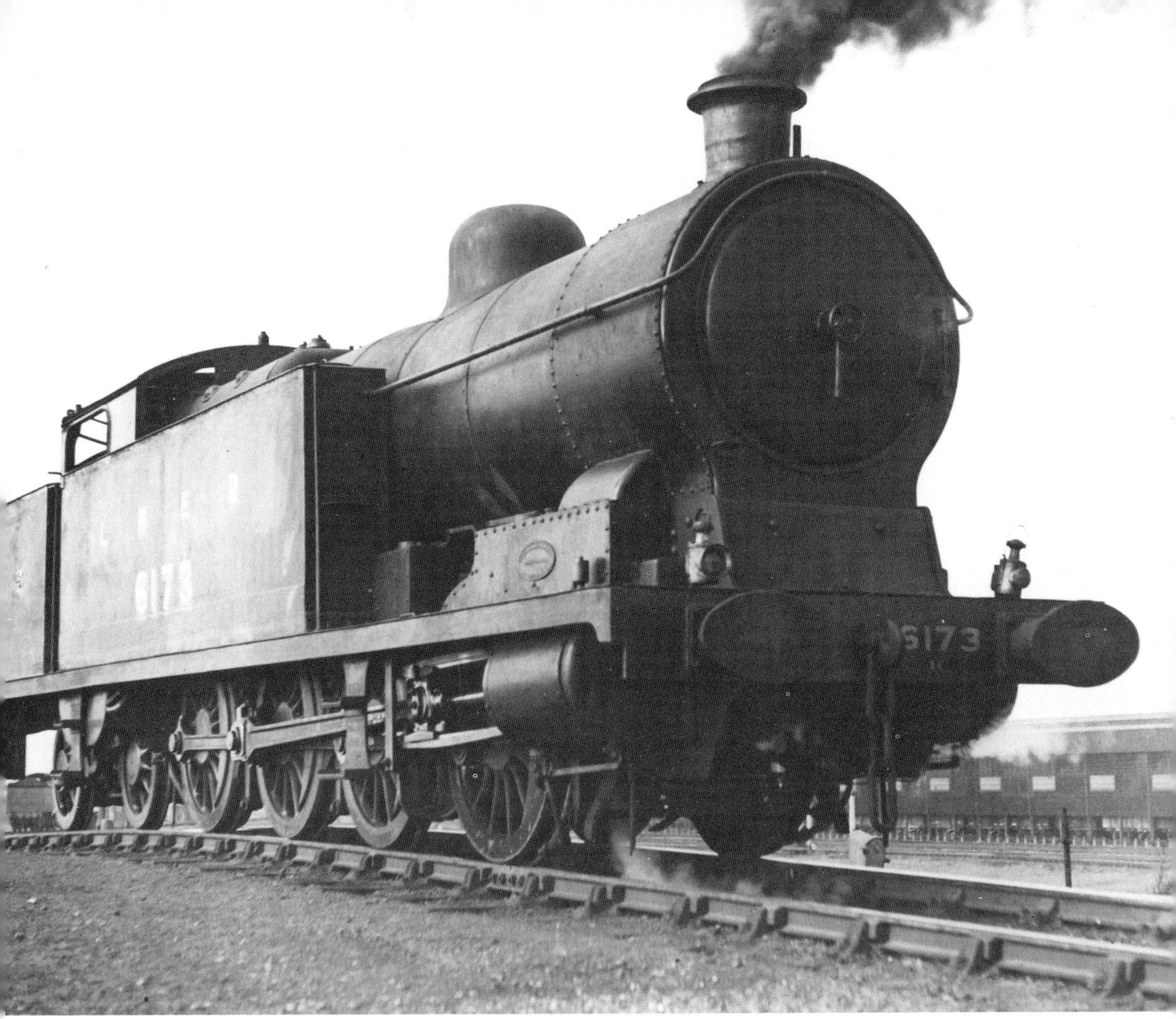
6173
6173

1171
GREAT CENTRAL

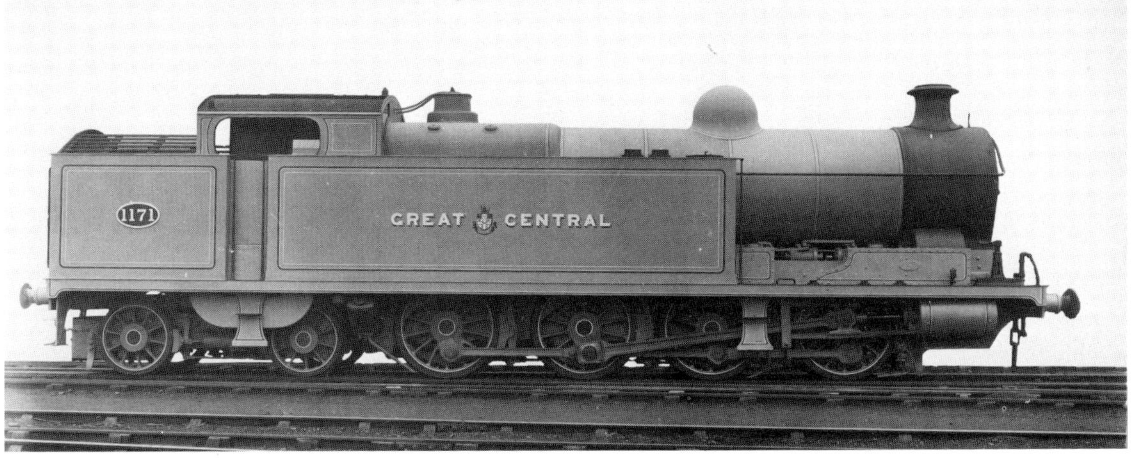

the period 1932-51. The use of the boosters ceased about 1940 and the equipment was removed in 1943.

The engines were built as follows:

GCR	Nos 1170/1	Beyer, Peacock	1907
GCR	Nos 1172/3	Beyer, Peacock	1908
LNER	Nos 2798/9	Gorton	1932

The LNER 1946 numbers were Nos 9900-5 in the above order.

When the new LNER diesel-electric shunters took over the work at March (in 1945) and later British Railways shunters took over at Wath (in 1953) it meant that these engines had little to do; attempts to make use of them at Frodingham, Immingham and Doncaster were not very successful and this resulted in their withdrawal.

Last of class withdrawn: 69901, 69905 (1/1957)
None preserved

The basic dimensions of the class were as follows:

	As built	*Superheated*
Heating surface, tubes		
Large and small (sq ft):	1,818	1,349
Firebox (sq ft):	154	151
Total (evaporative) (sq ft):	1,972	1,500
Superheater (sq ft):	—	242
Superheater elements:	—	22
Combined heating surfaces (sq ft):	1,972	1,742
Grate area (sq ft):	$26\frac{1}{4}$	$26\frac{1}{4}$
Tractive effort (lbs at 85% BP):	34,523	34,523*

* With booster in action: 46,896

Above right: The two Class S1 0-8-4Ts built by the LNER in 1932 were fitted with boosters to increase the tractive effort when 'cut-in'. The steam supply was taken from the smokebox (as seen in this view of No 2798) and then behind the right-hand side tank. Nos 2798/99 were built at Gorton, and had a number of standard Gresley fittings; with a GN-style chimney; side window cab; Ross 'pop' safety valves, and snifting valve behind chimney. Note the 'rake' of the front end of the side tanks, which carried less water than the GCR engines; but they took more coal. Coupling rod and balance weights on booster bogie clearly visible, also sandbox filler for bogie, under the letter 'L' of LNER at the base of the tank. *Photomatic*

Right: Another view of No 2798, just after renumbering in 1946 as No 9904, with the curious little Gill Sans numerals that were used at the time, and without the letters NE or LNER applied to the plain black livery. The booster had been removed from the bogie by this time, but the bogie retained the outside bearings. Photographed at Mexborough in August 1946. *A. F. Cook*

GCR Class 9N, LNER Class A5, BR Class 4P
4-6-2T Passenger Tank Engines
Introduced: 1911
Total: 45

The largest of Robinson's passenger tank engine designs made its first appearance in 1911, and this was intended for the growing suburban traffic out of Marylebone. The class remained on these duties until displaced by new Thompson 'L1' class 2-6-4T, in early British Railways days. Robinson at first considered a 4-6-4T scheme which Gorton prepared, as well as the 4-6-2T actually built.

These engines were the first of Robinson's classes to be built with superheaters, the first eight had the Schmidt type but his own version was used on the rest. The Schmidt type were replaced by the latter in due course. The second and later batches were built with larger superheaters, which then became the standard. The boiler was the same design as that used when the 4-4-0 '11B' class was converted to '11D', in 1913-26. In 1921 No 451 was modified with a side window cab, the first GCR tank so fitted; the others were altered similarly in 1924-6.

Ten engines were on order at the time of the Grouping and these consequently appeared in LNER apple green livery in 1923. No 5088 of this batch took part in the 1925 Stockton & Darlington Railway centenary celebrations. A further 13 were ordered by the LNER directors and Gresley countenanced their construction, for work in the North Eastern area. These were numbered amongst the former NER engines. This batch conformed to the LNER loading gauge and had reduced coal and water capacities. The cylinders were of the type that Gresley fitted to his LNER 0-6-0 'J38' and 'J39' classes, with longer valve travel, but with smaller diameter piston valves. The wheelbase was lengthened by 4in, and the whole engine was $3\frac{1}{2}$in longer. For service in the north-east they were equipped with automatic air brake equipment in addition to vacuum ejectors, and they at first had the Raven fog signalling system, but this was removed before long. Later the air brake fittings became redundant and these were also removed. Like the GCR built engines, water pick up gear was fitted; this was removed from all engines by British Railways.

The engines were built as follows:

GCR	Nos 165-70, 23/4, 447/8	Gorton	1911
GCR	Nos 449-52, 128/9	Gorton	1912
GCR	Nos 371-4, 411	Gorton	1917
LNER	Nos 3, 6, 7, 30, 45/6, 88, 154/6/8	Gorton	1923*
LNER	Nos 1712/9/38/50/6/60/5-8	Hawthorn, Leslie	1925†
LNER	Nos 1771/82/4/90	Hawthorn, Leslie	1926†

** These engines appeared as No 3, etc, lettered LNER*
† Numbered in the North Eastern section stock.

With the exception of Nos 5447 (a premature withdrawal) the class was renumbered 9800-42 in the 1946 scheme.

Below: GCR Class 9N, LNER Class A5 4-6-2T design. Illustrated is a later diagram showing side window cab, top feed to boiler and Ross 'pop' safety valves.

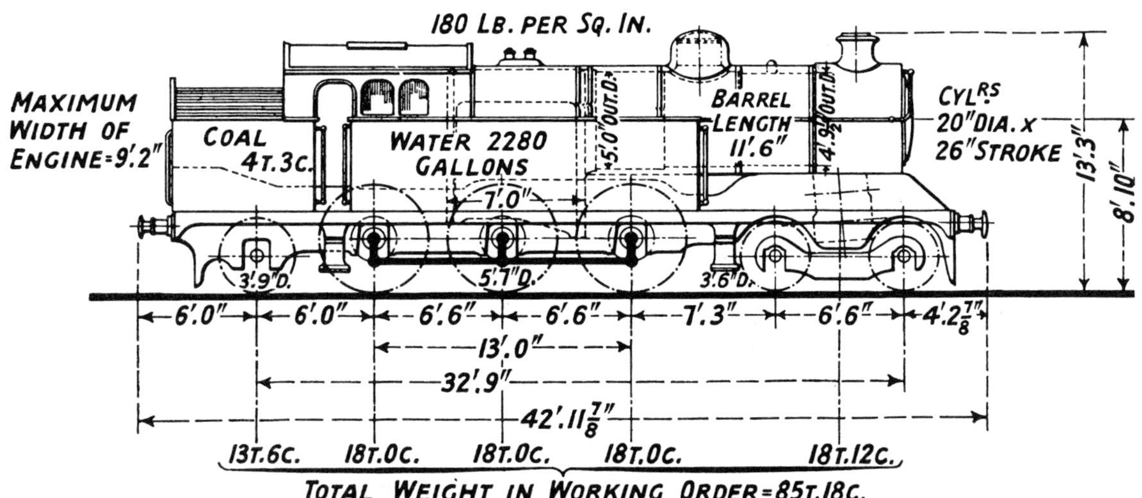

All the engines built by the GCR and also the 1923 batch, were stationed at Neasden, some being fitted with 'Reliostop' signalling equipment in 1919-21. To combat the coal shortage of 1921 Nos 23/4, 128/65/6/8, 371-4 were fitted for oil burning, and of these Nos 5023/4, 5165/6, 5372/3 were fitted again in 1926-7. The engines sent to the north-east generally remained there, apart from a few that spent some months at Norwich in 1951. Those displaced from Neasden became more scattered and were used in the Nottingham, Lincolnshire and East Anglian areas, until withdrawn in the late 1950s.

Last of class withdrawn: 69820 (11/1960)
None preserved

The basic dimensions of the class were as follows:

	1911 batch	*Standard*
Heating surface, tubes		
Large and small (sq ft):	1,238	1,139
Firebox (sq ft):	141	141
Total (evaporative) (sq ft):	1,379	1,280
Superheater (sq ft):	145	178
Superheater elements:	18	22
Combined heating surfaces (sq ft):	1,524	1,458
Grate area (sq ft):	21	21
Tractive effort (lbs at 85% BP):	23,743	23,743

Below: No 170, of the first batch of Class 9N 4-6-2Ts delivered from Gorton in 1911. Full GCR passenger green livery was applied to these large and handsome passenger tanks. Polished brass casing surrounds the four safety valves fitted. Inward sloping coal cage on bunker to permit good visibility when running bunker first; no windows to cab side. *Ian Allan Library*

Right: What an immaculate engine to carry one to one's daily toil in the City! An unidentified Class 9N 4-6-2T is seen in a positively gleaming state as it hurries a Marylebone suburban train along near Neasden. *Ian Allan Library*

Below right: Top feed apparatus was added by Robinson to some boilers, ahead of the dome, as seen here on Class 9N 4-6-2T No 128 of the 1912 Gorton batch. No steam heating hose carried on front bufferbeam during the summer months. For their time of introduction these were a remarkably large and powerful type of suburban tank engine by British standards. *LPC*

GREAT CENTRAL

Above: In 1926/27 six engines were for the second time fitted for oil-burning (10 having been fitted-out in 1921) and one of these, No 5165 is seen here, with the oil tank prominently sited in the bunker. Additional features of interest in this picture are the side window cab; the top feed; the Ross 'pop' safety valves; the superheater header discharge valve on the smokebox side, and the 'Reliostop' mechanical brake gear fitted alongside the trailing coupled wheel. Although lettered and numbered in the LNER series, and painted black, the engine carries full GCR style lining-out. *LPC*

Below: The LNER perpetuated the Robinson 4-6-2T design, which became their Class A5, when some new passenger tank engines were required for the North Eastern area. Gresley, the new CME wisely recognised the abilities of the design, and apart from reduced height boiler mountings and reduced coal and water capacities, there was really little changed (see text for further details). Visually the different chimney and squat dome were not an improvement, and there was a slight

alteration to the shape of the upper surface of the main frames under the boiler at the front end. Illustrated, in shop grey livery when new, is No 1784 built by Hawthorn Leslie in 1926. *Ian Allan Library*

Above right: Side windows to the cab, and twin Ross 'pop' safety valves are the chief differences noticeable in this picture of No 5024, in LNER lined black livery. Steam heating hose carried below front bufferbeam. Behind the engine is an immaculate Gresley brake third, and another brings up the rear of the train. *E. R. Wethersett*

Below right: During a serious shortage of engine power at Stratford, on the GE Section, in 1951 10 of the LNER-built batch were drafted to the GE suburban services. The GCR-built engines could not be used due to their greater loading gauge. BR No 69832 (ex-LNER No 1738) was photographed passing beneath the Ilford flyover with a down Southend train on 21 April, 1951. All was returned to the north-east in the summer of the same year. *R. E. Vincent*

Right: The distinctive bunker design of the big Robinson tank engines is well depicted in this picture of BR No 69803 (ex-No 5168) taken at Mablethorpe in September 1954. Behind the engine is a former GNR quad-art set of distinctly vintage appearance. The Class A5s worked on several former GNR branches in the east Lincolnshire area.
P. H. Wells

Below: The lined black livery of BR days quite suited the massive form of the Robinson 4-6-2Ts, as can be seen in this study of No 69827 (ex-No 5154) standing at Grantham station in July 1958. This type of engine was used on the Nottingham-Grantham services after displacement from Neasden. For a while, late on in their days, one example found its way on to the Kings Cross empty stock workings.   *P. H. Groom*

GCR Classes 8K & 8M*, LNER Classes 04 and 05* (also 01† by rebuilding), BR Class 7F and 8F†
2-8-0 Heavy Goods Engines
Introduced: 1911, 1918* & 1944†
Total: 666 (grand total of engines built)

If Robinson had produced no other design of locomotive he would still have secured his place in history with these engines, for they became more widespread than any other British class, and were certainly amongst the best known. In the United Kingdom the only areas where they were not seen at some time or other were the North of Scotland, Mid-Wales and the Southern Railway, although they had earlier made a limited appearance on both the London and South Western and the South Eastern & Chatham Railways.

During 1910 several ideas for a new heavy goods engine were considered, such as 2-8-2 and 2-10-0 locomotives, and for a 2-8-0 in both inside and outside cylinder form. The latter was adopted, the first engine appearing in 1911 and due to its size and type, the class inevitably became known as 'Tinies'. Basically the '8K' was a superheated version of the '8A' 0-8-0, having pony wheels to support the greater front end weight and to produce a smoother ride. Construction for the GCR was concentrated in 1911-4, totalling 126. As World War 1 dragged on the Military authorities had the problem of finding sufficient motive power for army traffic in France, and they began by borrowing about 600 existing locomotives from Britain's railways, including the GCR. Then the Ministry of Munitions chose the '8K' class for large scale construction, the first appearing in August 1917.

In 1916 plans for fitting a larger boiler were prepared, and two years later the '8M' version appeared, 19 of which were completed by 1922. The boiler was 6in greater in diameter, but otherwise they were similar to the '8K', class apart from the last nine having a side window cab. Class 8M also included No 966, the very first engine of the class, which was fitted with the larger boiler in 1918. On the other hand, in 1922 two '8M' engines were fitted with the smaller boiler and became '8K' class engines. Robinson used four of the class in experiments with pulverised coal and 'colloidal fuel' (60% pulverised coal and 40% oil), starting with No 353 in 1917. This engine was modified so that the special fuel was induced into the firebox, through two holes of $7\frac{1}{2}$in diameter, where it was supposed to mix with the combustion air. In practice the firebox volume proved too little for satisfactory mixing and the equipment was later removed. Next Robinson had No 422 altered to burn pulverised coal, in 1919, and a special double bogie tender carrying 7 tons of coal and 4,000gal of water was attached. Then No 420 was altered in 1920 to burn the colloidal fuel. A further experiment commenced in 1921 when No 966 was fitted with an even bigger boiler, of 6ft diameter, which was round topped and had a special firebox and grate. Fuel and 33% combustion air entered as a flat layer, and were immediately enveloped in the remaining air supply drawn in by the blast, becoming a violent turbulent mixture which ignited spontaneously. This engine also acquired the special tender from No 422. Nos 420 and 422 were tested against the unaltered No 419 between Dewsnap Sidings (near Gorton) and Dunford (east of Woodhead). Tests with No 966

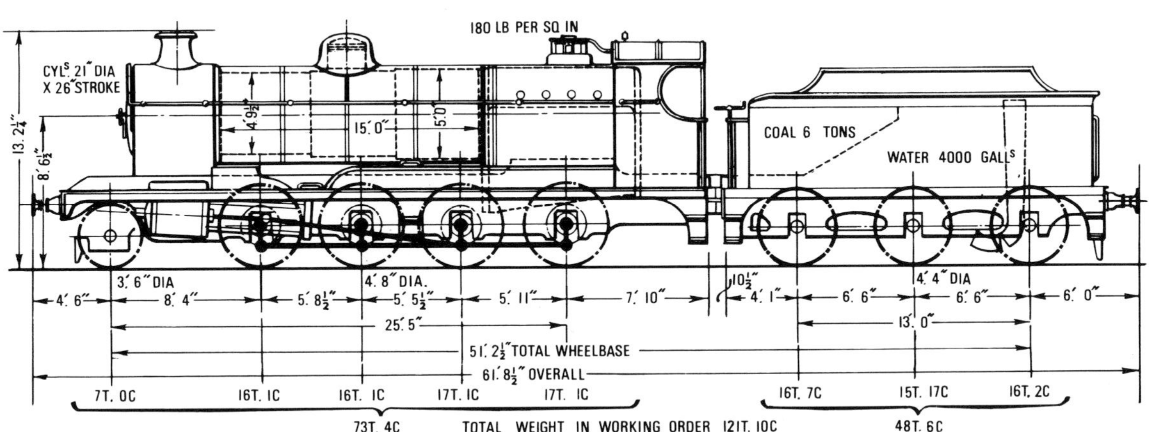

Above: The straightforward clean lines of the Robinson Class 8K 2-8-0 design — the 'Tinies' as they were so often called — are shown to advantage in this North British Locomotive Co official photograph of No 1209, built in 1913, and finished in lined-out workshop grey for photographic purposes. No GCR coat of arms carried on either engine or tender.   *Mitchell Library.*

Below: The first of four 'Tinies' fitted-up for trials with alternative fuels, No 353 was converted to burn 'colloidal fuel' in 1917. The tank for the special fuel was mounted upon a specially modified tender; the most noticeable features being the wider gap between the cab and the tender front, and the removal of the tender coping, or coal guard. The engine has top feed apparatus and no casing to the safety valves. *LPC*

Right: The larger-boilered version of the 2-8-0, the Class 8M, of which No 420 is illustrated. This particular engine was another one converted to burn 'colloidal fuel', in 1920. The tender (which has the GCR coat of arms) was not extensively altered and retained the standard body with the fuel tank fitted in the coal space. The boiler has top feed and twin Ross 'pop' safety valves and the Robinson superheater header discharge valve is on the side of the smokebox. Note the additional horizontal handrail carried on the smokebox door of this engine. *L&GRP courtesy David & Charles*

GREAT CENTRAL
420

Above: The most drastically altered engine was No 966 when fitted in 1921 for lengthy trials with the 'colloidal fuel'. A special larger diameter boiler with a unique round-top firebox, and a side-window cab gave the engine a different look, and was dramatically emphasised by the immense double bogie tender. After the experiments had ceased, the tender body became an oil storage tank at Gorton, and the bogies were used in the construction of a well wagon. *LPC*

continued as well but in February 1924 they were abandoned, it being stated officially that despite proving successful in use as fuel, the cost of preparation and handling was prohibitive.

The GCR acquired three of the six engines built at Gorton in 1918-9 to Government order and put them into stock as Nos 1, 5 and 8. At the Grouping the company possessed 148 2-8-0 locomotives of which 130 were '8K' class, 17 '8M' class and the other No 966 with its special boiler, which it lost in 1924. Whilst not the most numerous class on the LNER at the time it was destined to achieve that distinction by reaching a total of 421 with the purchase of surplus Government engines.

The choice made by the Ministry of Munitions when it placed orders for the construction of 344 engines for military use in France proved to be a good one. Gorton was to build 25 of these, but in fact only six were built. As World War 1 drew towards its end, a further 196 engines were ordered on Cabinet authority, so that there would be further work for two firms of locomotive builders. The first engine for France was ready in August 1917, and the speed of construction was such that by February 1919 no less than 305 had

been sent across the English Channel. At first they were transported by ordinary ships but in February 1918 the Richborough train ferry service was started and that became the normal route. Construction continued until the end of 1919, when a total of 521 had been completed and if one adds the 145 others built to GCR orders, this places the class amongst the most numerous ever built in Britain.

As soon as the war ended the existence of so many quite new military locomotives became a problem. There was an immediate attempt to sell the engines, and this met with a modest initial success. Three were taken into stock by the GCR in May 1919 which in fact had never left Gorton, and in official circles these are not recorded as delivered so that the total in such sources is given as 518. The GWR took 20 that month, and the LNWR was negotiating for 30, when sales were stopped, it being decided instead to hold the locomotives in a 'pool' of Government rolling stock, from which all at some time in the period 1919-22 were taken on loan by several of Britain's railways. Only the GWR held on to any when the end of Government control came in August 1921. Gradually all the engines were put to store in Government sidings, at Aintree (29), Beachley (64), Gretna (50), Morecombe (41), Queensferry (198), Royds Green (33), and Stratton (53). Of those on loan to the LNWR 30 had been purchased by that railway in November 1920, which left a total of 468 still as Government property.

Many attempts were made to sell the Government engines, but for years the asking price was too high, reaching as much as £12,000 in 1921. The Government expected to get the new price, despite the wear and tear they had suffered! It was not until March 1923 that any further sales took place and it took four years to clear the lot as follows:

Date	No	Purchaser	Price per loco (£)
3/1923	3	J. & A. Brown	Not known
12/1923	125	LNER	2,000
2/1925	48	LNER	1,500
3/1925	3	J. & A. Brown	2,000
5/1925	80	GWR	1,500
7/1925	12	Arnhold & Co	2,000
7/1925	3	J. & A. Brown	1,800
10/1925	6	Arnhold & Co	1,230
10/1925	6	Arnhold & Co	2,050
11/1925	3	J. & A. Brown	1,200
12/1925	2	Arnhold & Co	800
2/1927	100	LNER	340
3/1927	75	LMS	340
3/1927	1	J. & A. Brown	1,000

The LNER batches became Nos 6253-6377, 6495-6542 and 6543-6642 respectively. Sixteen of these LNER engines were altered for use in Scotland, having the overall height of the chimney, dome and cab roof reduced, and were put to work on the Fife to Aberdeen coal trains, becoming Class 04/2. The engines concerned were Nos 6286/8/90/1, 6328/46/51/2/70/2, 6543/4/8/50/1/82.

Top: Externally the '8K' design was virtually unaltered when built for ROD service, except for the fitting of the automatic air brake, with the pump situated on the right hand side of the smokebox. Detail changes were the provision of carriage warming apparatus (for hauling troop trains) and the two side chains on the engine and tender bufferbeams, to comply with continental requirements. However, a major technical change not visible, was the use of steel instead of copper for the firebox. Twin Ross 'pop' safety valves fitted and cast iron numberplate on cabside. Illustrated in works grey finish is No 1951 built by North British in 1918. *Mitchell Library*

Above: Another experiment was the application of Caille Pottonie feed-water heating system in 1922, to No 1234. This had the heater exchanger mounted below the footplate, with a prominent pipe running alongside the boiler to the smokebox. Top feed casing on boiler, and brass casing to safety valves. *Ian Allan Library*

Above right: 'Somewhere in France' is this ROD 2-8-0 No 1841. The extra bufferbeam fittings are clearly visible also the two rerailing jacks carried on the front end. 305 of the type served in France. Nos 1601-32/47-95, 1701-24, 1801-1959/72-99 and 2002-4. The first arrived there in the autumn of 1917 and the last in February 1919. Most were 'repatriated' in 1919; only a few remaining abroad until 1920.
P. Rowledge collection

Centre right: ROD No 1859 in trouble in France, possibly due to a collision which has severed the left hand cylinder and ripped off the running plate and one buffer. The board at the top of the smokebox in front of the chimney indicates that the engine was allocated to Dunkirk depot.
Imperial War Museum

Below: On loan to the GCR, after return from Europe, ROD No 1927, still in original livery and with the air brake, is seen heading a train of empties. The numbers loaned were: 50 to the Caledonian, 93 to the GCR, 44 to the GER, 84 to the GWR, 181 to the LNWR (who purchased 30 in 1920) and 33 to the North Eastern. The LYR had 27, the LSWR had 17 and the SECR had six, for a while, but all these were transferred to the GWR and LNWR and are included in the above totals. *Real Photographs*

Few classes of locomotives in Britain have suffered from so much rebuilding, producing a further five variations for no other reason than using Doncaster round top boilers instead of making more Belpaire boilers (which seemed to be anathema to Gresley), or later in order to produce Thompson's standard postwar goods class. Despite this, some engines of the original design served their lives virtually unaltered until the end of the active use of the class in 1966! The variations introduced by this succession of rebuilding were as follows:

Class 04/4	Two engines fitted in 1929 with GNR 2-8-0 boilers which necessitated lengthening the frames.
Class 04/5	Nine engines fitted in 1932-9 with the same boiler as '04/4', apart from having a shorter barrel to avoid lengthening the frames.
Class 04/7	41 engines altered in 1939-44 again using the GNR boiler, but with the barrel shortened even more so that the original smokebox could be retained.
Class 01	Rebuilding to Thompson's design of 58 engines in 1944-52 as part of his new range of standard locomotives, using the new boiler which had been designed for his 'B1' class 4-6-0 and new cylinders with outside Walschaerts valve gear.
Class 04/8	Fitting of the same boiler type to 98 engines in 1944-58.

(Some engines suffered more than one of the above rebuildings).

Above: The nine larger-boilered Class 8M engines built in 1920-22; Nos 10-15/7/9/22, differed from all the other 'Tinies' in having the attractive side window cab. This feature was retained when the LNER later converted them to Class 04/6. No 17, illustrated has top feed and Ross 'pop' safety valves. *P. Rowledge collection*

The class was initially to be found in use over the greater part of the GCR system, but later the LNER made more widespread use of them. In addition to those sent to Scotland, they were to be found on the former Hull & Barnsley, the GN&GE joint line and at GNR sheds at Ardsley, Colwick, Grantham and New England. In postwar years the type was allocated almost entirely to former GCR depots. One major exception was the fitting of five of the '01' variety with air pumps and equipment for working the air-powered hopper doors of the wagons used on iron ore trains between Tyne Dock and Consett.

With the outbreak of World War 2, and once again an urgent need to find suitable motive power, the Government requisitioned 92 in 1941 as described below. These were all written-off the stock book at the end of 1943, but it was not until February 1947 (ie two years after the end of the war) that the LNER received a payment of £524,000 for them. As all 92 were still in LNER stock when the 1943 renumbering scheme was prepared the blocks of numbers included all of them; the groups of numbers allocated (sorted into builder and order of construction) were as follows, renumbering actually taking place in 1946-7:

Nos 3500-3625	GCR '8K' class
Nos 3626-8	ROD built at Gorton and taken into GCR stock
Nos 3629-42	ROD built by Nasmyth, Wilson
Nos 3643-69	ROD built by Kitson
Nos 3670-3734	ROD built by R. Stephenson
Nos 3735-3901	ROD built by North British
Nos 3902-20	GCR built as '8M' class

The numbers allotted to those engines which were sent overseas remained blank, until those between Nos 3572 and 3809 were used again, when it was necessary to renumber for a second time. Thus 59 between 3500 and 3569 were renumbered again because their numbers were needed for the LNER-owned LMS type '8F' 2-8-0 engines which themselves had to be renumbered to make way for the 200 'Austerity' or 'WD' 2-8-0 which were purchased in December 1946. All that it seems to prove is that the careful sorting of the renumbering scheme did not really matter that much!

The '8M' version of the class (LNER '05') took a long time to disappear (from 1922 to 1943) and was re-classified '04/6' on being provided with the smaller boiler of the '8K' class (those with side window cabs retained them). A further reduction in numbers took place in 1952 when five were sold to the War Department and were sent out to their Suez base. General withdrawal commenced in December 1958 and the last of the former LNER engines were condemned in April 1966, having worked until then in the Doncaster area.

Having acquired in all 100 of the surplus Government engines the GWR initially renumbered the 80 purchased in 1925 to 3020-99, following the 20 obtained in 1919 which were Nos 3000-19. Almost immediately the batch of 80 was put aside and then thoroughly sorted so that 30 were fully overhauled and renumbered 3020-49. The other 50 were returned to traffic renumbered 3050-99 and ran only until heavy repairs were needed; the last being scrapped in 1931. The other 50 engines lasted until 1947-58.

The engines purchased by Arnhold were reconditioned by Armstrong, Whitworth at Newcastle, and modified for use by Chinese railways. This encouraged the disposers to believe that there was a market overseas after all, despite their failure to sell any abroad when first put up for sale. Engine No 1615 was therefore given a special overhaul in 1926 as a demonstrator, but the move was unsuccessful and it was in fact the last engine to be sold. In contrast, No 2137, which had been damaged when on loan to the Caledonian Railway, was cut up in 1926 to ascertain the scrap value!

The engines sent to China served with three public railways and a colliery line belonging to the Kailan Mining Administration. Virtually nothing is known of their subsequent history, but one was

Below: A statistical curiosity is that the LMSR were the second largest owners of Robinson locomotives, having 105 in its possession for a few weeks in the summer of 1927! LMSR No 9654, seen here at Crewe in June 1929, started life as ROD No 1832, ran as LNWR No 2929 in 1919-21, became LMSR No 9654 in 1927, and was condemned as their No 9418 in 1932. All spent their LMSR working life on the Western Division, usually north of Crewe and in North Wales. Note the LMSR power classification of 7F on cabside and the brackets for the air pump on the smokebox side, which has been replaced by the vacuum brake. *H. C. Casserley*

Above: The LNER rebuilding by Gresley, to Class 04/5 of some engines was detrimental to the fine lines of the original Robinson design. The typical Doncaster style smokebox and chimney seemed to sit very uneasily upon the front end. No 5008, seen here, was one of the three completed by Gorton as ROD Nos 2005-7, but never delivered. They were taken into GCR stock in 1919, but the company did not in fact buy them; the accountants wrote them in at cost value and the government never paid for their construction! *Real Photographs*

observed by an Australian enthusiast in 1954, on the quayside at Shanghai when he was working as a seaman.

The LMS was more interested in having the tenders than the actual engines and used only 20 of the 75 purchased in 1927. Many of their tenders ran for years attached to former LNWR engines, and some tenders lasted even longer in departmental use. Thirty of the surplus engines were sold to Armstrong, Whitworth during 1927 and 22 then went to China (the other eight being broken up in 1933), while the balance of 25 was scrapped in 1927-30. Two of these engines had the shortest working life of any of Robinson's engines, only from the beginning of 1920 until August 1921!

The engines purchased by J. & A. Brown were for use on their colliery line in New South Wales; known as the Richmond Vale Railway. The three purchased in 1923 were modified by the removal of the superheaters and retubing. These arrived in Australia in 1926, followed by the other 10 in 1927, all being transported in Brown's own vessels. In fact there was never a time when all 13 were at work together as it was not until 1933 that the last engine was put into use, by which time another engine had ceased working. Brown's engines worked for the last time on 28 June 1973, and these were the last working examples of Robinson engines, having outlasted the BR examples. Three are preserved.

The 92 engines requisitioned by the Government in 1941 consisted of 31 ex-GCR and 61 ex-ROD locomotives. They were despatched, from September 1941 until January 1942, to the Middle East. In fact a start had been made on requisitioning no less than 300 for use in France in 1939, only a few being prepared, but none actually went as it was decided to build LMSR Stanier '8F' engines instead. Two of the Robinson engines were lost on the voyage, but all the rest served in Egypt and Palestine and on the Haifa-Beirut-Tripoli line, which was then under construction. Sent out as WD Nos 700-91 they became Nos 9700-91 and then in September 1944 Nos 70700-91. In 1945 seven (Nos 70724/46/7/56/71/86/91) were moved to Iraq, and all but No 70746 passed into Iraqui stock; these were withdrawn in 1955.

With the return of peace most, if not all, of the remaining engines passed into Egyptian hands, and then ran with the 97xx series numbers. In 1952 the War Department purchased five more of the class from British Railways and sent them to the

Suez base as Nos 040-4 (ex-LNER Nos 6222, 6615, 6215, 5069 and 5005 respectively). When the British left Suez in 1954-5 they passed into Egyptian hands as Nos 9794-8. In Egypt the Robinson engines appear to have lasted until the early 1960s.

With such a complex history it is of benefit to the reader to separate the building details, as follows: The GCR orders for Class 8K totalled 126, and were built as follows (GCR numbers):

Nos 966, 26, 69, 93, 331-5	Gorton	1911
Nos 102/33/55, 346-55, 400/2-8	Gorton	1912
Nos 1183-1202	Kitson	1912
Nos 1203-50	North British	1912
Nos 1251/2	North British	1913
Nos 375-85	Gorton	1913
Nos 386-99, 271	Gorton	1914

In addition three built at Gorton in 1919 for ROD service became GCR Nos 1, 5 and 8 (see below).

The 19 Class 8M engines were built as follows (GCR numbers):

Nos 412-5/7-9	Gorton	1918
Nos 420-2, 10-13	Gorton	1919
Nos 14/5/7	Gorton	1920
Nos 19, 22	Gorton	1921

In the preparation of the LNER renumbering scheme the above 126 engines were allotted numbers 3500-3625 in the same order, but those that were to have become Nos 3512/20/3/30/2/43/4/9/51/9/64/72/7/80/2/5/6/94/8, 3600/1/7/8/17/25 were by then overseas and were never renumbered as intended. The remainder that took numbers between 3500 and 3569 were again altered in 1947, becoming Nos 3572/7/80/2/5/6/94/8, 3600/1/7/8/17/25/32/4/5/40/3/54/8/60/4/9/71/7/8/80/3/4/90/2/3/8, 3700/7/10/1/9/22/3/7/36/8/43/5/57/61/2/72/3/7/8/89/97/9, 3803/5/9 respectively. The 19 engines built as Class 8M became Nos 3902-20, apart from the six taken by the WD; leaving the Nos 3903/9/10/6/8/9 blank.

The 521 engines built to Government orders were (ROD numbers) as follows:

Nos 1601-32	Kitson	1918
Nos 1633/5/6/8/40-6	Stephenson	1919
Nos 1647-50	Stephenson	1918
Nos 1651-64	Stephenson	1917
Nos 1665-90	Stephenson	1918
Nos 1691-1700	Stephenson	1919
Nos 1701-4	Nasmyth, Wilson	1917
Nos 1705-24	Nasmyth, Wilson	1918
Nos 1725-32	Nasmyth, Wilson	1919
Nos 1733-49	Stephenson	1919
Nos 1787-1800	North British	1919
Nos 1801-41	North British	1917
Nos 1842-1960	North British	1918
Nos 1961-71	North British	1919
Nos 1972-91	North British	1918
Nos 1992-2001	North British	1919
Nos 2002-4	Gorton	1918
Nos 2005-7	Gorton	1919*
Nos 2008-13/5-31/3-44/6-8/51-84/6-99, 2100-67	North British	1919

* *Did not run as ROD Nos 2005-7, but were put into service as GCR numbers 1, 5 and 8, becoming 3626-8 in the LNER 1946 renumbering scheme.*

Below left: ROD No 1794 became GWR No 3050 at first, in 1925 (having previously worked on the GCR during 1919-21), and then No 3020 when that year's purchase of 80 was sorted out in 1926-7. Seen here in BR black livery, No 3020 was photographed just past Stratford-on-Avon racecourse station, with the SMJR Stratford to Broom line on the overbridge in the background; in August 1952. The 2-8-0s boiler had been modified to Swindon standards, complete with brass safety valve casing and GWR type top feed, and a Swindon pattern chimney has been fitted.   *B. England*

Above right: Robinson's 2-8-0s had the distinction of serving in both world wars, and of going much further afield in the second one. Oil-burning WD No 70714 (built as GCR No 1183) is seen here at the head of an interesting formation of military traffic, south of Beirut on the Haifa-Beirut-Tripoli line, in July 1945.
R. E. Tustin

Below: In military service for the second time, WD 2-8-0 No 9789 has a distinctly unkempt appearance and has lost the boilerside handrail, but nevertheless was capable of some good work as an oil-burner. No 9789 was originally ROD No 1921 and then became LNER No 6603, before requisitioning. R. A. Riddles, whose job it was to find suitable engines for war use, considered requisitioning the entire class, but abandoned the idea because of the number of non-standard variations by then in existence. He chose instead the Stanier Class 8F 2-8-0 of LMSR design, and then finally produced his own 2-8-0 and 2-10-0 Austerity types for war use.
Imperial War Museum

Last of class withdrawn: LMSR 9460 (10/1933), GWR(BR) 3011/5/24 (10/1958), LNER(BR) '8K' 63612 (11/1965), '01' 63828 (8/1965), ex ROD 63858 4/1966
Examples preserved: Britain: GCR No 102 (BR 63601). Australia: J & A Brown (NSW) Nos 20, 23 re-numbered as 21) and 24.

The basic dimensions of Classes 8K and 8M were as follows:

	'8K' as built	'8K' standard	'8M' as built
Heating surface, tubes			
Large and small (sq ft):	1,457	1,349	1,641
Firebox (sq ft):	154	154	174
Total (evaporative) (sq ft):	1,611	1,503	1,815
Superheater (sq ft):	198	255	308
Superheater elements:	18	22	28
Combined heating surfaces (sq ft):	1,809	1,758	2,123
Grate area (sq ft):	$26\frac{1}{4}$	$26\frac{1}{4}$	$26\frac{1}{4}$
Tractive effort (lbs at 85% BP):	31,325	31,325	31,325

The LNER rebuildings were as follows:

	'04/4'	'04/5'	'04/7'	'04/8; 01'
Heating surface, tubes				
Large and small (sq ft):	1,869	1,795	1,755	1,493
Firebox (sq ft):	164	164	163	168
Total (evaporative) (sq ft):	2,033	1,959	1,918	1,661
Superheater (sq ft):	406	406	401	344
Superheater elements:	24	24	24	24
Combined heating surfaces (sq ft):	2,439	2,365	2,319	2,005
Grate area (sq ft):	$27\frac{1}{2}$	$27\frac{1}{2}$	$27\frac{1}{2}$	28
Tractive effort (lbs at 85% BP):	31,326	31,326	31,326	31,326*

* '01': 35,518lb

Left: The most numerous of the reboilered varieties of the LNER Class 04 2-8-0s was the 04/8 version, totalling 98. No 63858 (formerly ROD No 2064 and LNER No 6619) heads a down empty mineral train at Black Carr Junction, near Doncaster. *R. E. Vincent*

Above: The more shapely version of the LNER chimney, and a postwar Thompson-style dome cover give an improved look to No 63823 in BR days . The engine heads a coal train towards Ardsley through Lofthouse. In South Yorkshire the more usual nickname for the Robinson 2-8-0s was 'Superheaters', instead of 'Tinies' (which latter name referred to the '8A' class 0-8-0s in that area). *J. B. Welldon*

Below: Edward Thompson evidently admired the simplicity and strength built into his locomotives by Robinson, and when selecting existing locomotives as part of his new standard range for postwar LNER use, Thompson chose the Robinson two-cylinder 2-8-0 in preference to the Gresley three-cylinder type. Using the solid Robinson frames, Thompson placed his 'B1' 4-6-0 type boiler on them, and gave the engines new outside cylinders with outside Walschaerts valve gear. A 'B1'-type cab replaced the original, but Robinson's tender remained virtually unchanged. As LNER Class 01, a total of 58 engines was thus rebuilt between 1944-52. In BR days No 63687, (formerly ROD No 1669 and LNER No 6324) is illustrated on a train of empties. *Ian Allan Library*

Above left: Many of the class remained virtually unaltered to the end of their days, with just the reduced height boiler mountings required for wider use on the LNER. No 3710 (formerly GCR No 1194 and then LNER Nos 6194, and 3541 for a short time in 1946), was one such engine. The various Robinson gadgets and the top feed have been removed and a Gresley relief valve has been installed behind the chimney, but the basic engine is still pure GCR. No 3710, with wartime lettering NE on tender, and second 1946 number in small Gill Sans numerals, was photographed at Wentworth in April 1947.   *H. C. Casserley*

Left: From this angle there is precious little evidence of any Robinson features, except the tender, on Class 01 2-8-0 No 63856! Five engines were fitted in 1952 with air compressors for operating the hopper doors of the iron ore wagons which worked between Tyne Dock and Consett in Co Durham. The engines were Nos 63712/55/60, 63856/74.   *P. Ransome-Wallis*

Above: A picture that could easily have been taken somewhere in France during World War 1, but which was actually taken in New South Wales no less than 53 years after that war had ended! Only the lack of the air pump on the smokebox side, and the addition of an electric headlamp below the smokebox gives the game away. Brown's No 15 (ROD No 1889), takes water at Hexham exchange sidings in November 1971. The box on the front end above the main frames housed the battery for the headlight.   *Leon Oberg*

Above: Another of Brown's engines, No 13 (ex-ROD No 2119) gets away from Stockrington colliery with coal for the New South Wales Government Railway exchange sidings at Hexham. Little has been changed on the engine since its ROD days. The header discharge valve is still on the smokebox side, likewise the pair of side chains and the original type buffers on the bufferbeam. The air brake and carriage warming equipment has been removed, and an electric headlight added.   *Leon Oberg*

Left: With its original Robinson chimney sadly cracked, and bound together with a metal strap, Brown's No 23 (a Gorton-built engine ex-ROD No 2004) exhibits all the signs of a lifetime of hard work, as it stands preserved in New South Wales. The tradition persists that it was Brown's No 21 (ex-ROD No 1615) that hauled the Allied delegates to the signing of the Armistice on 11 November 1918 and accordingly No 23 has been retained in the guise of No 21. This is sadly inaccurate because it was, according to our researches a French 4-6-4T that hauled the train. Nevertheless its preservation is a fitting tribute to the tremendous war services of the Robinson 2-8-0s in both 1914-18 and 1939-45.   *J. Costigan*

SECTION 15

GCR Class 1, LNER Class B2 (later B19)
4-6-0 Express Passenger Engines
Introduced: 1912
Total: 6
'Sam Fay' class

The express passenger class produced during Robinson's inside-cylinder phase, of 1911-4, certainly looked impressive enough, and it seems that much was expected of it because the first engine was named after the General Manager, Sir Sam Fay, thereby giving the class its popular name. Two features distinguished the class when new; these were the $21\frac{1}{2}$in diameter cylinders and the heating surface of the boiler which was exceeded only by Churchward's *Great Bear* for the GWR, at that time. The initial engine, No 423 was the first GCR express passenger engine to be built with a superheater, and it was planned that it would be exhibited at an International exhibition in Belgium. For this reason it was finished with a copper-capped chimney, but in the event it never went, and a model was sent instead.

The engines were built as follows (GCR numbers):

No 423	Gorton	1912
Nos 424-8	Gorton	1913

The numbers first allotted in the 1946 LNER scheme were 1472-7; however Nos 5423/5/7/8 became Nos 1490-3, the other two being withdrawn as Nos 5424/6

Below: GCR Class 1 inside-cylinder express passenger 4-6-0 design; the 'Sam Fay' class of 1912.

Sadly, the performance of these engines did not live up to Robinson's expectations, and before long they were displaced from their main line duties by the next express passenger class to appear, the 'Directors'. The main weaknesses in the design proved to be the layout of the piston valves, which being close together were served by rather tortuous steam passages, and also the shallow firebox and restricted ashpan. In addition the arrangement of tubes, and the size of the superheater did not prove to be satisfactory, and two further layouts were tried before the Grouping; one enlarged the superheater from 24 to 28 elements, together with a reduction in the cylinder diameter to 20in. One further problem resulted from the big inside cylinders which made it impossible to provide adequate coupled wheel bearings, causing overheating troubles.

In 1921 Nos 423/4/6-8 were equipped for oil burning and, apart from No 427, were again so fitted in 1926-7.

After their displacement by the 'Directors' some of the class spent a short time at Immingham; otherwise they were stationed at Gorton until 1929. Thereafter they lived out their days at Sheffield and Immingham, on rather more humble duties than the top expresses for which they had been designed.

Last of class withdrawn: 1492 (11/1947)
None preserved

The basic dimensions of the class were as follows:

Heating surface, tubes	
Large and small (sq ft):	2,210
Firebox (sq ft):	167
Total (evaporative) (sq ft):	2,377
Superheater (sq ft):	440
Superheater elements:	24
Combined heating surfaces (sq ft):	2,817
Grate area (sq ft):	26
Tractive effort (lbs at 85% BP):	22,700

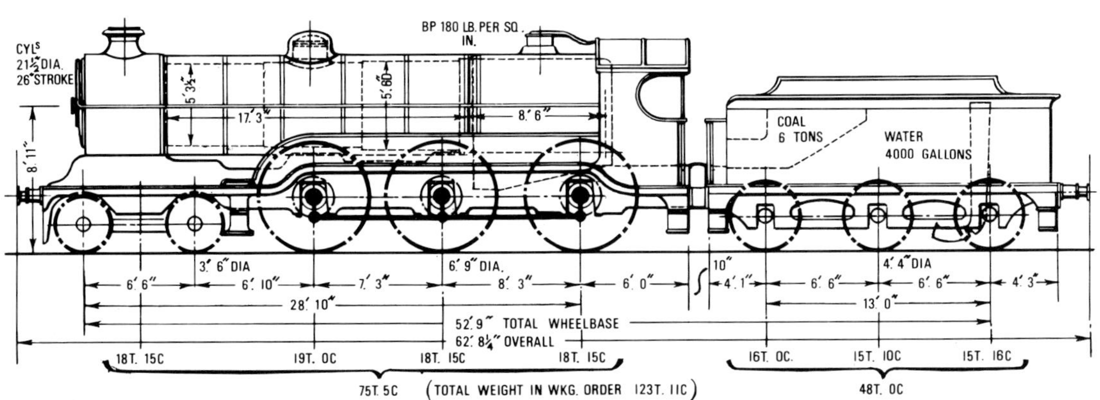

Above: The first engine of the Class 1 express passenger 4-6-0 type was No 423, which was named after the GCR General Manager, *Sir Sam Fay*. Pictured here in workshop grey livery, the bold lines of the inside-cylindered design are clearly seen. The chimney had a copper cap (see text), intended for exhibition purposes. *Ian Allan Library*

Right: Sir Sam Fay again; this time as an oil-burner during 1921, and seen leaving Marylebone on a down express in positively immaculate condition. The big tank for the oil fuel is just within the load gauge, and is seated in the coal space of the tender. Note the burnished buffers. *LPC*

Below: In positively gleaming condition, with all the exposed brass and metal trim highly polished, No 428 of Robinson's Class 1 express passenger 4-6-0s, named *City of Liverpool*, receives the attentions of the fireman in the tender, prior to departure. This class introduced a new look to Robinson's designs; as well as reverting to the use of inside cylinders. The new look was exemplified by the big continuous splasher over the coupled wheels, with the straight nameplate neatly incorporated in the brass heading which surrounded the splasher. *Ian Allan Library*

Below right: Another view of the first Class 1 4-6-0 No 423 *Sir Sam Fay*, taken whilst the engine was carrying a front end indicator shelter, during trial runs. It seems that the design did not come up to Robinson's expectations, and it was most significant that whereas the first three built had full GCR passenger green livery, the other three were delivered in the goods engine livery of black, lined red and white. *LPC*

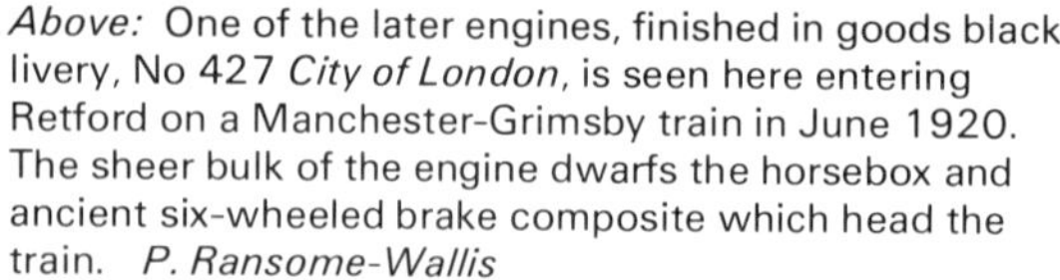

Above: One of the later engines, finished in goods black livery, No 427 *City of London*, is seen here entering Retford on a Manchester-Grimsby train in June 1920. The sheer bulk of the engine dwarfs the horsebox and ancient six-wheeled brake composite which head the train.   *P. Ransome-Wallis*

Right: Remarkably little changed, except for the small dome and later LNER chimney, and removal of the nameplates, No 1492 (ex-LNER No 5427 *City of London*) is seen just seven months before it was withdrawn from service as the last example of the class; photographed at Grimsby Town in April 1947.   *H. C. Casserley*

Below: Substitution of a 'flowerpot' chimney, and the Gresley-type snifting valve added to smokebox side, are two visible signs of LNER ownership, plus the lettering and number on the tender. Here No 5423, *Sir Sam Fay* in full apple green passenger livery, and retaining the original boiler and large dome is seen on an Immingham-Manchester train leaving Worksop in 1926. The engine had been converted to oil fuel for the second time in its career.   *P. Ransome-Wallis*

GCR Class 1A, LNER Class B8, BR Class 5MT
4-6-0 Mixed-Traffic Engines
Introduced: 1913
Total: 11
'Glenalmond' Class

The 'Glenalmond' class of 1913-5 was a small-wheeled version of the 'Sir Sam Fay' class, to which it bore a strong resemblance, and they were normally used on goods traffic, together with some slower passenger work and excursions. Not unexpectedly, they proved to have the deficiencies that had been exhibited by the previous class. Apart from the boiler arrangement changes, already described for the 'Sir Sam Fay' class, these engines were little altered and only two acquired the smaller 20in cylinders. These engines were the first to have Robinson's top feed when new, except the first one, No 4, which was fitted later.

Three, Nos 279, 443/5, were fitted with oil burning equipment in 1921, but unlike the other two, No 443 did not revert to coal in 1921, instead being used in connection with the colloidal fuel experiments until 1923.

Four were named, the first after the Scottish residence of the company's chairman, No 439 after a director and the other two after contemporary British military leaders.

The class was built as follows (GCR numbers):

No 4	Gorton	1913
Nos 279, 439-46	Gorton	1914
Nos 280	Gorton	1915

The allotted LNER numbers were 1331-41, but they became Nos 1349-59 in the above order.

Right: Fitted for oil-burning, when this picture was taken in 1921, with the large fuel tank prominently located on the tender, No 279 *Earl Kitchener of Khartoum* is illustrated in GCR lined black goods livery. The small coupled wheels of 5ft 7in diameter meant that the top line of the continuous splashers was only just in line with the top of the main frames at the leading end, giving a rather down at heel look to these fast freight engines. *LPC*

Below: Class 1A (LNER Class 8B) 4-6-0 mixed-traffic design.

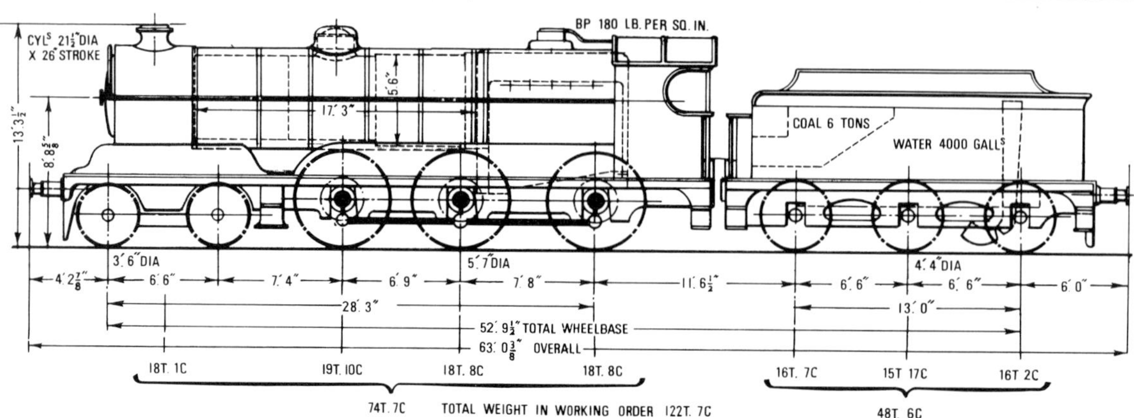

Left: With the tender lettered LNER and carrying the number 441, the locomotive is in a hybrid livery, because the GCR numberplate is still carried on the cabside. It is pictured here on a west-bound freight leaving Worksop. Robinson superheater header discharge valve clearly visible on the smokebox side, and top feed on the boiler. *P. Ransome-Wallis*

Below: As with most of Robinson's engines the Gresley LNER chimney, the smaller dome and the snifting valve on top of the smokebox did nothing for their appearance. The top feed remains on the boiler, but the Robinson superheater header discharge valve has been removed. In LNER black, lined red, goods engine livery No 5004 *Glenalmond* (first of the class) is illustrated. *LPC*

When new the class was divided between Gorton, Neasden and Immingham, but for 10 years after World War 1 Gorton and Annesley were their usual homes. Following this they spent their time at Colwich, where whilst handling excursion trains they reached a wide range of destinations. During the war *Glenalmond* was observed at Edinburgh, when it was certainly not on a pleasure trip.

Last of class withdrawn: 1357 (4/1949)
None preserved

The basic dimensions of the class were as follows:

Heating surface, tubes	
Large and small (sq ft):	2,020
Firebox (sq ft):	163
Total (evaporative) (sq ft):	2,183
Superheater (sq ft):	24
Superheater elements:	294
Combined heating surfaces (sq ft):	2,477
Grate area (sq ft):	26
Tractive effort (lbs at 85% BP):	27,445

GCR Class 11E and 11F*, LNER Class D10 & D11*, BR Class 3P
4-4-0 Express Passenger Engines
Introduced: 1913, 1919*
Total: 45

'Director' and 'Improved Director'* classes

Robinson must have been taken aback by the fact that this new 4-4-0 class of 1913 had to be utilised on the fastest expresses, because the 'Sir Sam Fay' class had shown its faults so quickly. Nor would he have, in all probability, have thought that they would come to be held in the greatest admiration, above all his other express locomotives. His thoughts for a new 4-4-0 certainly went back to 1908-9, when two schemes were prepared, and the ultimate result was a remarkable engine which proved both economical and fast. The secret of the success of the design lay in the size of the firebox, in relation to the boiler barrel. This was the same as that in the 4-6-0 engines, but of course the latter was shorter and so achieved a far better steam raising capability. All 10 engines were named after directors of the company, but No 429 suffered two changes of name, as listed in Appendix 2.

A further five of the class appeared in 1920, followed by another six in 1922, being 'Improved Directors', Class 11F. In all major respects the two classes were identical, except for the side window cabs. The names were more varied, being those of two directors, three royalty and six of the land and sea battles of World War 1. At this time, and much further north, the directors of the North British Railway were leaving in abeyance renewal of engine power, knowing that this could be handed over as a problem for the new LNER company, after the Grouping. So, as a direct result of this the LNER inherited an urgent need for new locomotives in that area. Construction of more of the 'Improved Directors' was agreed to by Gresley and in 1924 12 were built by Kitson and 12 by Armstrong, Whitworth; all being named in 1925 after characters in Sir Walter Scotts' 'Waverley' novels.

The engines of these two classes were built as follows:

'11E'	GCR	Nos 429-38	Gorton	1913
'11F'	GCR	No 506	Gorton	1919
'11F'	GCR	Nos 507-10	Gorton	1920
'11F'	GCR	Nos 501-5/11	Gorton	1922
'D11/2'	LNER	Nos 6378-89	Kitson	1924
'D11/2'	LNER	Nos 6390-6401	Armstrong, Whitworth	1924

The LNER 1946 numbers were 2650-94 in the above order.

Right: A question of aesthetics seems to have arisen when Robinson unveiled his first 'Director' class 4-4-0 at Gorton in 1913. As seen here, in this workshop grey photograph, No 429 *Sir Alexander Henderson* was first completed without coupling rod splashers, with a raised running plate similar to that featured on the 'Sam Fay' class 4-6-0s. Evidently someone in high authority disliked the naked aspect of the coupled wheels, and as the next illustration shows, coupling rod splashers were stipulated (and added to No 429 before it entered service.) *A. B. MacLeod Collection*

Below right: Complete with coupling rod splashers, 'Director' class 4-4-0 No 438 *Worsley-Taylor* is seen when just completed, in workshop grey livery; last of the original 10 Gorton-built engines of 1913. *A. B. MacLeod Collection*

Below: The drawing depicts one of the later LNER ordered engines, with reduced height boiler mountings; snifting valve behind chimney, side window cab and raised running plate over the coupled wheels without coupling rod splashers.

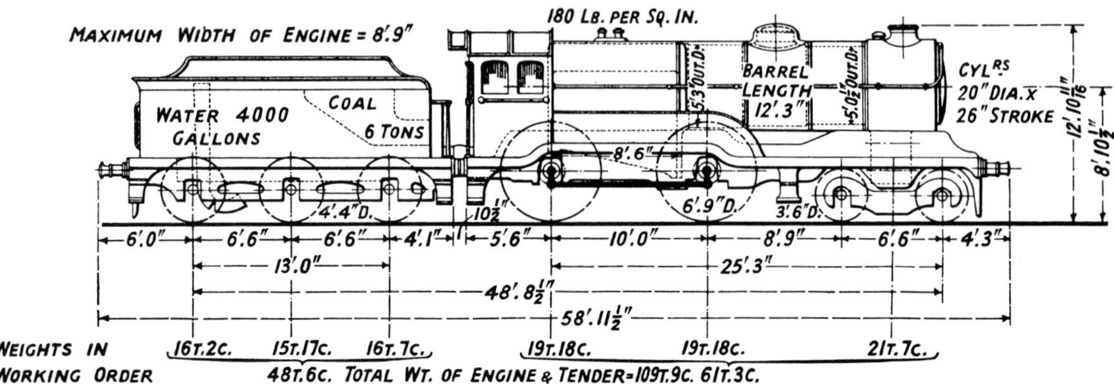

The 'Directors' made an immediate impact on the 1913 railway scene and established a reputation that was never tarnished. Their work on the GCR Main Line is even today the subject of discussion and admiration. Apart from the various Gresley modifications, the only major change in their appearance was the removal of the coupling rod splashers. After the Grouping some of the class put in an appearance on the GN section, working expresses out of Kings Cross, but many ended their days on Cheshire Lines services. The Scottish engines always remained north of the Border.

Last of class withdrawn: '11E' 62653 (10/1955); '11F' 62685 (1/1962)
Example preserved: GCR No 506 *Butler-Henderson* (BR No 62660).

The basic dimensions of the two variations of the class were as follows:

	'11E'	'11F'
Heating surface, tubes		
Large and small (sq ft):	1,502	1,388
Firebox (sq ft):	157	155
Total (evaporative) (sq ft):	1,659	1,543
Superheater (sq ft):	304	209
Superheater elements:	24	24
Combined heating surfaces (sq ft):	1,963	1,752
Grate area (sq ft):	26	26
Tractive effort (lbs at 85% BP):	19,645	19,645

Above: First of the class, No 429 *Sir Alexander Henderson* pictured again; this time in the original condition in which it entered traffic, in 1913, complete with coupling rod splashers.   *LPC*

Below: The sparkling condition in which GCR engineman kept their locomotives is beautifully portrayed in this study of 'Director' class 4-4-0 No 433 *Walter Burgh Gair*. Come to think of it, the idea of naming locomotives after the directors of the company was in itself a stroke of genius, calculated to ensure that their humble GCR employees kept their directors' namesakes clean and in good working order!   *Ian Allan Library*

Top: Of particular interest is this study of Class 11E 'Director' 4-4-0 No 429 *Sir Alexander Henderson*, working hard near Abbey Lane, Leicester, because attached behind the tender is the GWR 'Royal Train' in all its glory, making a splendid picture. *V. R. Webster*

Above: Fortune was to smile upon Class 11F 'Improved Director' 4-4-0 No 506 *Butler Henderson* one of the 1920 Gorton-built engines, because it survived to be preserved by British Railways. Seen here in its original GCR guise, the engine shows the side window cab and twin Ross 'pop' safety valves which characterised the '11F' variety. *LPC*

Above: 'Improved Director' Class 11F 4-4-0 No 501 *Mons* is seen leaving Marylebone at the head of an express, when these engines were the prime motive power of the GCR main line; showing themselves capable of performances equal to the Robinson 4-6-0 designs, and with a greater economy.   *LPC*

Below: The early days of the Grouping produced some locomotive livery and numbering oddities such as is seen here on Class 11F (LNER Class D11) 'Improved Director' No 504. Still in GCR passenger green livery, complete with oval cabside numberplate, the tender nevertheless carries the full initials of the new parent company: L.&.N.E.R. (note the full stops and the ampersand) and the number is painted on the tender. Just to confuse things still further, the GCR coat of arms is still on the splasher beneath the nameplate *Jutland.*   *LPC*

Below: A batch of 'Improved Directors' was built by the LNER as their Class D11, for service in the former NBR area of Scotland. By this time Robinson had retired, to make may for the younger Gresley as first CME of the new company, and one can only hazard a guess at who it was that decreed that these engines should revert to Robinson's original design, with a raised running plate over the driving wheels and no coupling rod splashers; but one suspects it was Gresley. Finished in full apple green passenger livery, and with the reduced height chimney and dome needed for the NB loading gauge, No 6394 *Lord James of Douglas* made a very handsome picture. *LPC*

Above: The Scottish engines had their names painted on the splashers and did not have the brass beading. Class D11 No 6401 *James Fitzjames* is seen here in LNER black livery. The 'Improved Directors' were not all that popular on the NB lines because of their right hand drive. *A. Swain collection*

102

Above left: Removal of the coupling rod splashers certainly gave the ex-GCR engines the more modern look that Robinson had at first envisaged. Here is LNER No 5437 of Class D10 renamed *Prince George* and seen at the head of the 4.55pm express from Marylebone, at Preston Road in 1934, with a complete rake of Gresley carriages behind the tender. LNER style chimney, and black livery with red lining. *Real Photographs*

Left: Probably at no time in British locomotive history, (except for perhaps the last few months of steam) did the locomotive stock look so run down and forlorn as it did in the immediate post World War 2 years. The condition of No 2664 *Princess Mary*, seen here at Neasden in April 1947 was all too typical of this difficult phase. No one could even be bothered to keep the brass nameplate legible *H. C. Casserley*

Above: Scottish Class D11 4-4-0 No 62686 (ex-No 6393) *The Fiery Cross* presents a dramatic picture as it leaves Thornton on the 6.32pm to Edinburgh in August 1952; with the engine painted in BR lined black livery, and the leading Gresley brake third in the carmine red and cream colours. *W. J. V. Anderson*

Above: BR No 62692 (ex-No 6399) *Allan-Bane*, looking somewhat the worse for wear, at Haymarket shed in October 1955. The engine is in the black mixed-traffic livery with LNWR-style lining, but note that the splasher has only a single red line around it.   *John Robertson*

Below: The enlightened directors of the Northern Rubber Company chose a 'Director' class 4-4-0, No 62666 (ex-No 5502) *Zeebrugge* to head an NRC special train. The headboard, numberplate and shedplate have all been decorated with a pale blue background, and the engine shows the benefits that careful grooming could bestow upon the lined black BR livery.   *E. R. Wethersett*

Above: Passing through Padgate station on the CLC, near Warrington on 17 October, 1953 is BR No 62663 (ex-No 5509) *Prince Albert*, on a down Class H through freight for the Manchester area. In their final days some of the 4-4-0s were in plain black livery, as seen here.   *E. D. Bruton*

Left: A somewhat inglorious end befell Scottish 'Director' No 62685 *Luckie Mucklebackit* when central heating facilities were urgently required by the Caledonian Hotel, Edinburgh. By courtesy of Morfitts the Plumbers (as the sign on the boilerside tells us), the engine became a stationary boiler, complete with sacks of coal alongside. Robinson, we feel, would *not* have approved of the chimney!   *H. Malhan*

GCR Class 1B, LNER Class L1 (later L3), BR Class 5F
2-6-4T Freight Tank Engines
Introduced: 1914
Total: 20

In view of the later popularity of the 2-6-4T for passenger work in Britain it perhaps is surprisng that, apart from the two Leek & Manifold narrow gauge engines, there were no engines of this wheel arrangement in existence until 1914. These Robinson engines were intended for goods work and, unlike all others in Britain, had inside cylinders. The 0-6-4T 'D' class, inherited from the Lancashire, Derbyshire & East Coast Railway, formed the basis of the design, although a 4-6-2T version was also considered. In appearance the 2-6-4T followed the massive outline of all the later Robinson engines and the enginemen, forming their own judgement, called them 'Crabs'. The boiler was that already used on the 'Directors', modified with top feed and the bogie was exactly that of the 0-6-4T. The valve gear drove outside admission piston valves through rocking gear. The side tanks were wider than the cab and bunker, and in order to give rear end clearance the back buffer beam was reduced in width. Water pickup gear was fitted, located between the trailing coupled wheels and the bogie, but was later removed by the LNER.

The intention was to use these engines on export coal traffic from the Nottinghamshire and Derbyshire pits to Immingham, but only the first two were completed in 1914, before that traffic ceased. However construction of the remainder continued until 1917, as there was a need of them elsewhere, and there was still the possibility that the export coal trade might return to its prewar status once the war ended. The class was divided between Gorton and Sheffield in its early days, and then spread to other sheds, Neasden receiving a

Below: GCR Class 1B 2-6-4T (LNER Class L1) for freight duties; with inside cylinders.

Above right: Visually the Class 1B 2-6-4T was perhaps the least successful of Robinson's designs for the GCR, as there was something distinctly out of balance about the size of the cab, tanks and bunker in relation to the front end of the engine. Nevertheless they were impressive machines and when new they featured a lot of Robinson's patent gadgetry, including top feed apparatus, circulating valve and blower and anti-vacuum valves for each cylinder, the left hand one of the latter can be seen on the frames just ahead of the splasher. No 272, first of the class is illustrated in shop grey livery, lined out and lettered for photographic purposes. *LPC*

Right: Class 1B 2-6-4T No 276, as built. Note the coat of arms on cabside instead of between the words Great Central on the tank. Although intended primarily for goods traffic the engines had the vacuum brake fitted, and did some passenger work. *Ian Allan Library*

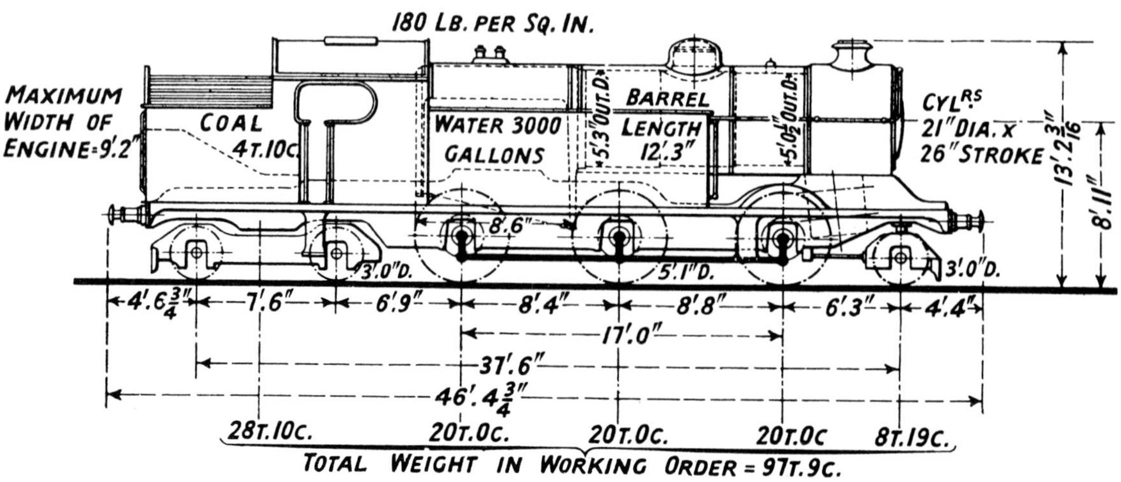

few which even did some passenger work. In their latter days there were several at Northwich, and the last few survived at Woodford until 1955.

The engines were built as follows (GCR numbers):

Nos 272/3	Gorton	1914
Nos 274-6, 336-40	Gorton	1915
Nos 341-4	Gorton	1916
Nos 345/66-70	Gorton	1917

The LNER 1946 renumbering was 9050-69 in the above order.

Last of class withdrawn: 69069 (7/1955)
None preserved

The basic dimensions of the class were as follows:

Heating surface, tubes:	
Large and small (sq ft):	1,388
Firebox (sq ft):	155
Total (evaporative) (sq ft):	1,543
Superheater (sq ft):	304
Superheater elements:	24
Combined heating surfaces (sq ft):	1,847
Grate area (sq ft):	26
Tractive effort (lbs at 85% BP):	28,759

Above: Gresley-era chimney and the removal of some of the fittings were signs of LNER ownership when this picture was taken of Class L1 (later L3) 2-6-4T No 5344 at Doncaster in April 1934. The engine is in black livery, and still retains the top feed and cylinder anti-vacuum valves. Ross 'pop' safety valves have replaced the originals, without the brass casing. *Photomatic*

Below: LNER Class L3 (reclassified to make way for the new Thompson L1 Class 2-6-4Ts) No 9055 (ex-No 5336) is seen here at Neasden in the company of an ex-Metropolitan Railway 2-6-4T No 6160. Both engines are in the wartime black livery, with abbreviated company initials NE on the tankside. Later style LNER chimney fitted, also Ross 'pop' safety valves and Gresley anti-vacuum valve behind the chimney. *H. C. Casserley*

Below: Photographed on a down goods train near Wendover in August 1950. Class L3 2-6-4T No E9056 (ex-No 5337) is in the early BR hybrid livery with E prefix to number and the words British Railways painted in Gill Sans lettering on the tankside. *E. C. Griffith*

Bottom: The final BR livery, of unlined black, had the locomotive number transferred to the bunkersides. The massive bulk of Robinson's 2-6-4Ts is well captured in this picture of No 69060 (ex-No 5341) on a down freight at Chalfont in July 1951. *P. Ransome-Wallis*

GCR Class 9P, LNER Class B3 (and B3/3*)

4–6–0 Express Passenger Engines
Introduced: 1917, 1943*
Total: 6

The largest of Robinson's express passenger engines first appeared as a solitary example in 1917 and was duly named after the then Chairman, Lord Farringdon. It was not until 1920 that the other five were built. Using the same boiler as the 'Sir Sam Fay' and 'Glenalmond' classes these new engines had four cylinders, with divided drive and Stephenson link motion. As the cylinders were in line, a rather unusual layout of the motion was needed, with the cranks of the adjacent inside and outside cylinders set at 180° to each other, and with their valves driven by the same eccentrics and rockers thereby causing the adjacent valves to move together, but in opposite directions. This meant that there had to be outside admission for the outside cylinder valves and inside for the inside cylinders. The cranks for the inside cylinders were set at 90°, so avoiding dead-centre problems and providing an even four beats per revolution. What would have been exceedingly long outside connecting rods were avoided, by using much longer than normal piston rods, and by placing the

crossheads and slidebars further back from the cylinders.

The engines were built as follows (GCR numbers):

No 1169	Gorton	1917
Nos 1164-8	Gorton	1920

Initially Nos 1480-5 were allotted in the LNER 1946 renumbering scheme, but the numbers used finally were 1494-9, although No 6168 was not actually renumbered.

Although avoiding some of the problems of the 'Sir Sam Fay' class these engines did not prove to be as successful as they deserved to be, and they were undoubtedly heavy on coal at times, although when well handled they could give top class performances. Short travel valves and the small grate were the reasons for their limitations. As a result, Gresley rebuilt four of them with Caprotti valve gear, Nos 6166 and 6168 in 1929, No 6167 in 1938 and No 6164 in 1939. This proved to be a successful alteration, showing, on average, a 16% economy in coal. The 1938-9 conversions had the later Caprotti arrangement with steam instead of spring operated valves. No 6166 underwent a second reconstruction in 1943 to become almost a new engine in reality, with a Thompson boiler and new front end frames. In effect it was a 6ft 9in coupled-wheel version of Thompson's own 'B1' 4-6-0 class. Only the tender remained to show the GCR ancestry.

Apart from the first and last engines, the names were associated with World War 1, three leaders, and the GCR War Memorial engine (No 6165 *Valour*) with specially inscribed nameplates.

When new No 1169 went to Gorton shed and the others were divided between that depot and Immingham, hardly an indication of praiseworthy

Below: Class 9P (LNER Class B3) four-cylinder express passenger 4-6-0 design of 1917.

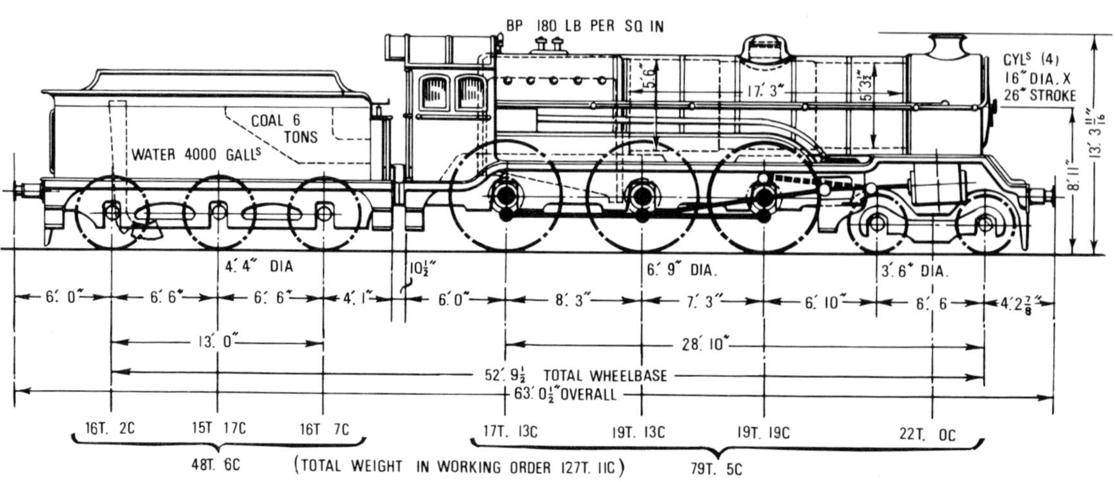

Above: Representing the ultimate in GCR express passenger engine design, Robinson's 'Lord Farringdon' class four cylinder 4-6-0, with an unusual layout of the valve motion, necessitated by the in line position of the four cylinders. No 1169 *Lord Farringdon* is seen in shop grey finish, when new. 'Reliostop' mechanical brake control system fitted to the tender between leading and centre wheels. *LPC*

Below: Robinson's Class 9P 4-6-0 No 1165 was selected as the GCR 1914-18 war memorial engine. Below the name *Valour*, the brass nameplate was inscribed: 'In memory of GCR employees who gave their lives for their country 1914-18.' Due to the size of the shield-shaped nameplates the oval Gorton building plates had to be fixed to the cylinder covers instead of in the usual position on the splashers. Until 1938 it was customary for *Valour* to work a special train from Manchester to Sheffield each Armistice day, for a special remembrance service to be held; the engine being suitably decorated. A design change on Nos 1165/7/8 was the provision of the new style side-window cab. *Ian Allan Library*

Above left: Leaving Marylebone with a down express in late GCR days, Class 9P 4-6-0 No 1169 *Lord Farringdon* is still in substantially original condition except for the substitution of Ross 'pop' safety valves. Note the tiny coupling rod splasher below the nameplate and worksplate, on the main continuous splasher; necessitated by the throwover of the outside connecting rods. *LPC*

Below left: At the head of the 10.0am down express from Marylebone, Class 9P 4-6-0 No 1167 *Lloyd George* is seen near Rushcliffe Halt. This engine had its name removed in 1923. As well as the Ross 'pop' safety valves, the engine also has the later side-window cab. The great length of the reversing lever was a feature of these big engines. *L&GRP courtesy David & Charles*

Above: The 1923 Grouping saw Robinson's Class 9P 4-6-0s and other classes moved to places further afield on the new LNER system. Still in GCR livery, the war memorial engine No 1165 *Valour* is seen here on the turntable in Kings Cross station yard. The GNR loading gauge was generous enough to take the '9Ps' without alteration to the boiler mountings. *LPC*

Below: To give them a wider route availability on the LNER system, the boiler mountings were reduced in height on the Class 9Ps, as on most other Robinson classes. With Gresley style chimney, snifting valve and squat dome, No 6167 is seen here in early LNER apple green livery, and after removal of the *Lloyd George* nameplates. The LNER classified the engines as 'B3'. *LPC*

Above: Mr (later Sir) Nigel Gresley, the LNER CME must have watched the performance of the Robinson engines running over ex-GNR metals with considerable interest; and of course, would have noted their heavy coal consumption. He chose two, Nos 6166/8 for rebuilding with Caprotti valve gear in 1929 and followed this with two more with improved Caprotti gear in 1938/39; these were Nos 6167 and 6164 respectively. No 6168 *Lord Stuart of Wortley* shows the first version. They became LNER Class B3/2, and a definite reduction in coal consumption was achieved.   *Photomatic*

Below: Photographed on a Manchester-Marylebone express near Darnall in 1927, Class B3 4-6-0 No 6166 *Earl Haig* still carries the original Robinson chimney but has a Gresley snifting valve on the smokebox side, and the later squat dome.   *P. Ransome-Wallis*

performance. In 1923 all six were transferred for service between Kings Cross and Leeds, but their work was not particularly impressive. Spells of GCR main line work followed, principally after rebuilding, but all finished up at Immingham or Lincoln, apart from No 6168 which was condemned from Neasden.

Last of class withdrawn: 1494/8 (12/1947)
None preserved

Typical basic dimensions for the engines were as follows:

	No 1169 as built	No 6166 Rebuilt 1943
Heating surface, tubes		
Large and small (sq ft):	2,020*	1,508
Firebox (sq ft):	163	168
Total (evaporative) (sq ft):	2,183*	1,676
Superheater (sq ft):	294*	344
Superheater elements:	24*	24
Combined heating surfaces (sq ft):	2,477*	2,020
Grate area (sq ft):	26	28
Tractive effort (lbs at 85% BP):	25,145	24,555

* Nos 1164-8 (as built) 1,881 sq ft, 2,044 sq ft, 343 sq ft, 28 and 2387 sq ft respectively.

Below: As in the case of the Robinson 2-8-0s, the successor to Gresley. Mr Edward Thompson, viewed the Class B3s as candidates for rebuilding with his standard components. Only one engine was reconstructed; in 1943. This was No 6166, which became Class B3/3, with new boiler, cab, outside cylinders and two sets of outside Walschaerts valve gear. Only the tender was true Robinson! Seen here at Neasden, the engine was in wartime black livery when photographed. One suspects this rebuilding was too costly to be worthwhile for the rest of the class. *C. C. B. Herbert*

GCR Class 8N, LNER Class B6
4-6-0 Mixed-Traffic Engines
Introduced: 1918
Total: 3

The solitary initial engine of this class appeared in 1918, amongst a batch of 8M 2-8-0s which had the same boiler, cylinders and motion; then two more appeared in 1921. The design seems to have been intended to eliminate the shortcomings of the 'Glenalmond' class, and this was an aim that was achieved, for they gained a reputation for free steaming and steady riding.

The boiler was of the same diameter as that used on Classes 1 and 1A, but being shorter had a smaller heating surface. The firebox was however deeper, and this proved to be a happy combination as far as the enginemen were concerned. Unlike the eight-coupled engines, these three engines retained this size of boiler, and were never significantly altered, although various minor changes were made in LNER days.

The engines of this class were built as follows (GCR numbers):

No 416	Gorton	1918
Nos 52/3	Gorton	1921

At first they were to have become LNER Nos 1328-30 in 1946 but they actually became Nos 1346-8 in the above order.

Below: Class 8N mixed-traffic 4-6-0 design of 1918; later LNER Class B6.

Right: With the leather hose of a water column suspended in the foreground, Class 8N mixed traffic 4-6-0 No 416 (first of the class built at Gorton in 1918,) is seen standing on shed. Note the small diamond burnished on the smokebox door by the enginemen; a simple evidence of pride in their locomotive. Earlier style standard Robinson cab without side windows, on this prototype engine, and superheater header discharge valve prominent on the side of the smokebox.
L&GRP courtesy of David & Charles

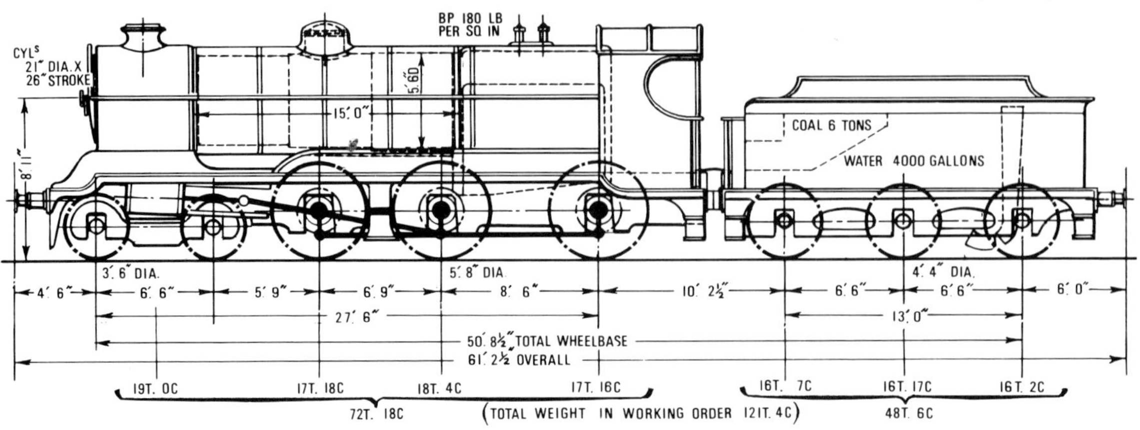

When new No 416 went first to Gorton and then to Neasden, but in 1921 all three were at Woodford. Later the LNER found plenty of work for them in the West Riding area, and they were at ex-GNR sheds for several years before they moved to Sheffield, in 1934. They spent their final months, in 1946-7 at Annesley.

Last of class withdrawn: 1347/8 (12/1947)
None preserved

The basic dimensions of the class were as follows:

Heating surface, tubes
Large and small (sq ft):	1,641
Firebox (sq ft):	174
Total (evaporative) (sq ft):	1,815
Superheater (sq ft):	308
Superheater elements:	28
Combined heating surfaces (sq ft):	2,123
Grate area (sq ft):	$26\frac{1}{4}$
Tractive effort (lbs at 85% BP):	25,798

Above: No 52, second of the three Class 8N engines, completed at Gorton in 1921 is seen here at the head of a Newcastle-Southampton through working formed of GWR stock, at Leicester in 1922. Note the vans bringing up the rear of the train. The second and third engines had the later standard cab, with side windows. Livery was the lined black of the GCR when new.
L&GRP courtesy David & Charles

Below: On a special working, with the reporting number 68 carried on the front of the engine and on the end of the leading brake vehicle, LNER Class B6 No 5052 (formerly No 52) is seen here, still substantially as built except for a lower dome. These engines had Ross 'pop' safety valves fitted when built. One can but feel sorry for the travellers in the antique six-wheelers behind the tender — small wonder that one or two are leaning well out of the windows! *P. Ransome-Wallis*

GCR Class 9Q, LNER Class B7, BR Class 6MT
4-6-0 Mixed-Traffic Engines
Introduced: 1921
Total: 38

When a need arose for further mixed-traffic engines, Robinson decided upon a small wheeled version of his 'Lord Faringdon' class rather than the alternative which was to build more of the '8N' class. As much as possible was kept standard with the former class, but the cylinders were more steeply inclined and the coupled wheelbase was shorter, although the total engine and tender wheelbase was the same as the passenger engines. While the layout of the motion was similar, the leading coupled axle was 6in further from the cylinders, which meant that connecting rods were longer, but this feature allowed some improvement in the arrangement of the valve gear between the frames. The shorter coupled wheelbase permitted the use of a deeper ashpan than had been possible on the express engines, also a rear damper door.

Twenty-eight engines were delivered to the Great Central, and these were destined to be Robinson's last new design. The first engine, No 72, was fitted with oil burning equipment on the 'Unolco' system when new, but only for the short space of three months. Ten more ordered by the GCR were completed in 1923-4, and these had reduced height boiler mountings and cabs to suit the LNER loading gauge. (The last two appeared with LNER numbers 5483 and 5484). The class very quickly gained a reputation for heavy coal consumption, and this earned them the title of 'Black Pigs' or sometimes 'Colliers Friends'. This heavy consumption was no doubt due to their short travel valves, but in fact they stood fair comparison with the other similar sized 4-6-0 engines which were inherited by the LNER. Despite this characteristic they were probably the best of the Robinson 4-6-0 classes, and they did the work for which they were intended very well, namely fast goods and relief and excursion trains. They proved to be fast engines despite the relatively small coupled wheel size.

The engines of this class were built as follows:

GCR	Nos 72/3/8	Gorton	1921
GCR	Nos 36-8, 458-64	Vulcan Foundry	1921
GCR	Nos 465-74	Gorton	1922
GCR	Nos 31-5	Beyer, Peacock	1922
LNER	Nos 475-82, 5483/4	Gorton	1923

All became Nos 1360-97 as intended in the LNER 1946 renumbering scheme, but 12 were affected by continuing deliveries of Thompson 4-6-0 engines, being altered as follows:-

Nos 5038, 5459/67/9/73/4 became BR Nos 61702-7
No 5034 allotted BR No 61708 (not altered)
Nos 5035, 5475/8/9/83 became BR Nos 61709-13

Below: GCR Class 9Q 4-6-0 mixed-traffic design of 1921; with the side window cab and top feed on the boiler.

Above right: In its original condition Class 9Q 4-6-0 No 461 displays the handsome final GCR appearance of Robinson's large engines, with top feed and Ross 'pop' safety valves. The extended outside cylinder piston rod is visible, supported by a guide just ahead of the footstep (which was incorporated with and partially obscures the slidebars.) The bridle rod's length made it necessary to fit a support at the front end of the long single splasher. *LPC*

Below right: The '9Q' class lived up to its mixed-traffic designation and was frequently used on excursion trains. No 33 heads one such train, again composed of vintage six-wheelers, plus one bogie clerestory, near Leicester when relatively new. *L&GRP courtesy David & Charles*

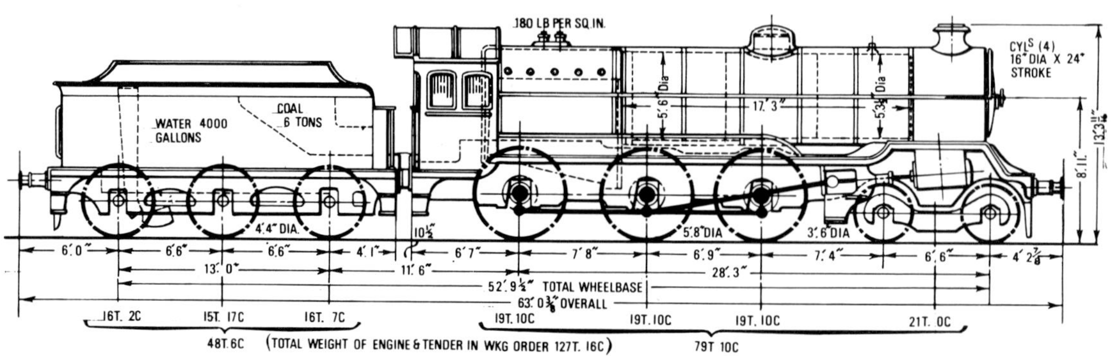

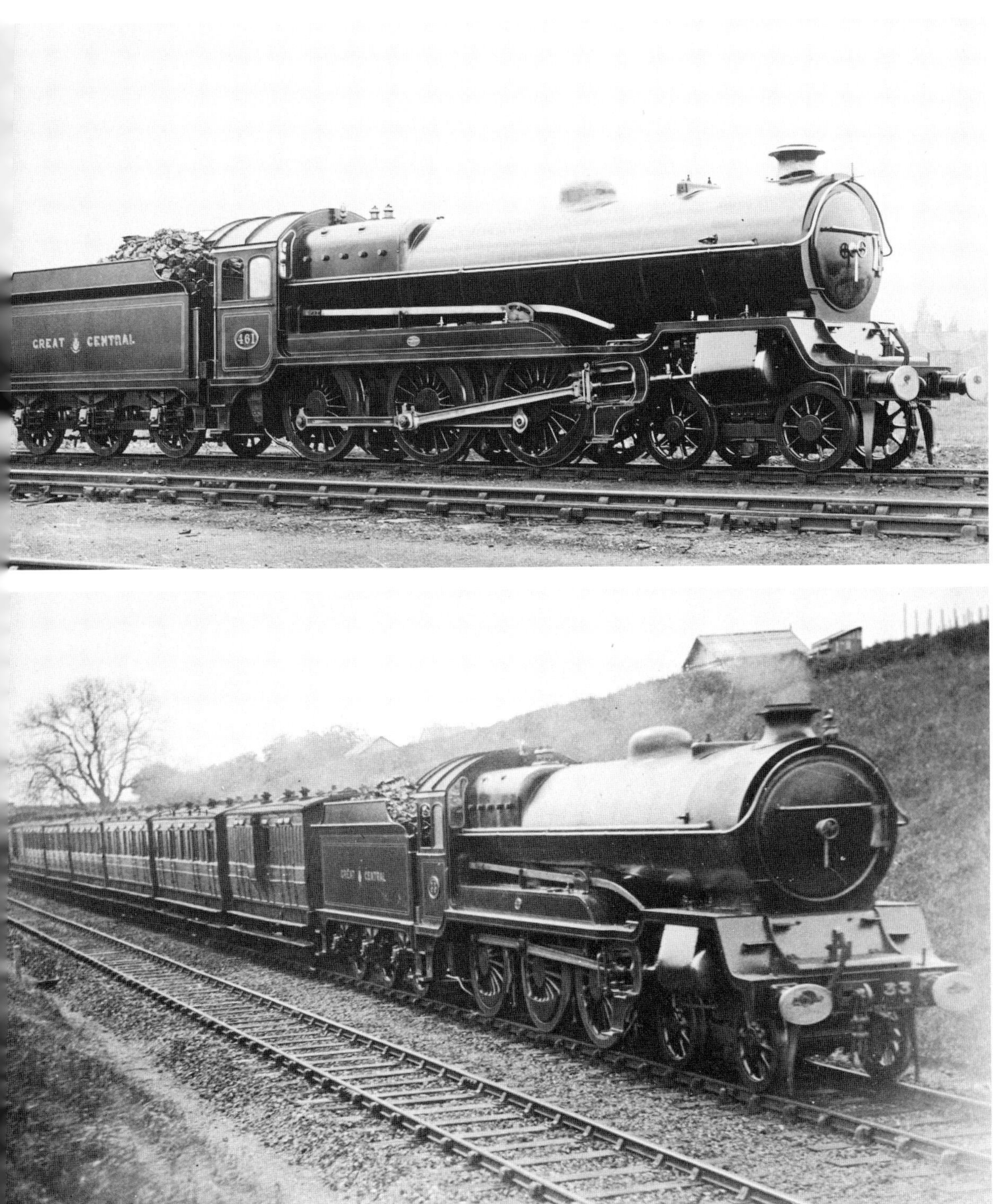

Left: Class 9Q No 72 initially ran as an oilburner, using Robinson's own system known as 'Unolco'. The oil tank is clearly visible in the tender. An interesting point about this picture of the engine making its very smokey exit from Marylebone, is that it is painted in unvarnished shop grey livery (except for the smokebox) and was presumably running-in on acceptance trials before final painting. *Ian Allan Library*

Above: With Robinson-style chimney, but with the top feed removed from the boiler, and a Gresley snifting valve on the smokebox top, LNER Class B7 4-6-0 No 5471 (ex-GCR No 471) is seen on express passenger duty sometime in the 1930s, passing South Ruislip & Northolt junction. *Real Photographs*

All the principal GCR sheds had examples of this class, with the majority stationed at Gorton for working the 'fitted' or 'piped' trains to such destinations as Marylebone, Grimsby, York or Liverpool. Due to the route knowledge of the drivers, in such links, they were also in demand for summer excursions to east coast resorts. Unlike the other GCR 4-6-0 classes, all 38 lasted long enough to become British Railways property; being withdrawn in 1948-50.

Last of class withdrawn: 61711 (7/1950)
None preserved

The basic dimensions of the class were as follows:

Heating surface, tubes	
Large and small (sq ft):	1,881
Firebox (sq ft):	163
Total (evaporative) (sq ft):	2,044
Superheater (sq ft):	343
Superheater elements:	28
Combined heating surfaces (sq ft):	2,387
Grate area (sq ft):	26
Tractive effort (lbs at 85% BP):	29,952

Above: The last new Robinson 4-6-0 engines appeared in 1923-24 and eight were delivered with the tenders lettered LNER, but with GCR numbers 475-82. All but the first two had the suffix C, to indicate Great Central section. However the last two appeared in 1924 as Nos 5483/4. For a short while a large cabside oval numberplate was used by Gorton, together with large numerals on the tender. No 481C became No 5481 in February 1924 and is seen here in this hybrid LNER livery. The height of the boiler mountings has been reduced to suit the composite LNER loading gauge.

Below: The large cabside numberplate seen in the previous picture was not a standard type, and Gorton soon came into line with the other LNER works in using a much smaller cabside plate. In this view of No 5475 the original position of the larger plate is still visible, with the much smaller plate now occupying the centre of the cabside. The initial LNER livery was black with red lining. *LPC*

Below: This broadside of No 5072 on the turntable at Neasden clearly shows the LNER modifications to the boiler, with the top feed removed, a smaller dome cover, Gresley snifting valve, but later, slim Robinson style chimney. *C. C. B. Herbert*

Bottom: Looking extremely run-down, the last of the class survived long enough to carry its BR number, 61711. The engine is seen standing at Gorton in April 1950; it was withdrawn four months later. All 38 engines had been renumbered in 1946-7 to the originally allotted 1946 numbers, unlike the other GCR 4-6-0 types. A few were further renumbered, however, in 1949 when their numbers were needed for new Thompson Class B1 4-6-0s, which overlapped in the 1360-1397 series. *W. H. Whitworth*

Appendices

1 Steam and Petrol-electric Railmotors

The Great Central was one of the participants in the use of steam railcars when these had a brief period of popularity on Britain's railways in the first decade of this century. Three were built at Gorton, No 1 in 1904 and Nos 2 and 3 in 1905. The engine unit was fitted within the body, which was 61ft 3in long, the rest of which was divided into a luggage compartment, a first class compartment, a vestibule, then a third class non-smoking saloon with a driving cab at each end. The first class (12 seats in No 1 and 16 in Nos 2 and 3) had longitudinal upholstered seats, the third (44 seats in No 1 and 34 in Nos 2 and 3) transverse reversible rattan covered seats. The entrance vestibules had collapsible gates and hinged steps, there being a valve in the vacuum brake pipe, oerated by linkage connected to the steps to prevent the creation of vacuum until the steps had been retracted.

The boiler was a multi-tubular vertical type mounted on the power bogie and the coupled wheels were driven by outside cylinders having Walschaerts valve gear. Water was carried in tanks under the frames between the bogies and coal in the boiler compartment. Controls were fitted at both ends and the conductor/guard could signal to the driver by means of electric bells. Electric lighting was fitted in the saloons, these being some of the first vehicles on the GCR so equipped.

First services worked by the steam rail cars were New Holland to Barton and Wrexham to Brymbo and Seacombe; later there was brief use between

Marylebone and South Harrow. Later still, when a public service was needed during the construction of Immingham docks, one of these steam cars ran on the Grimsby District line serving halts near Grimsby and Immingham. However, like the similar cars tried out on many other railways, they were never really popular with either the passengers or the operating staff and they were taken out of stock in 1921, having lain idle for some years beforehand.

During the summer of 1908 drawings were prepared for steam railcar No 4 but following a visit by the general manager to Hungary in 1910, ideas

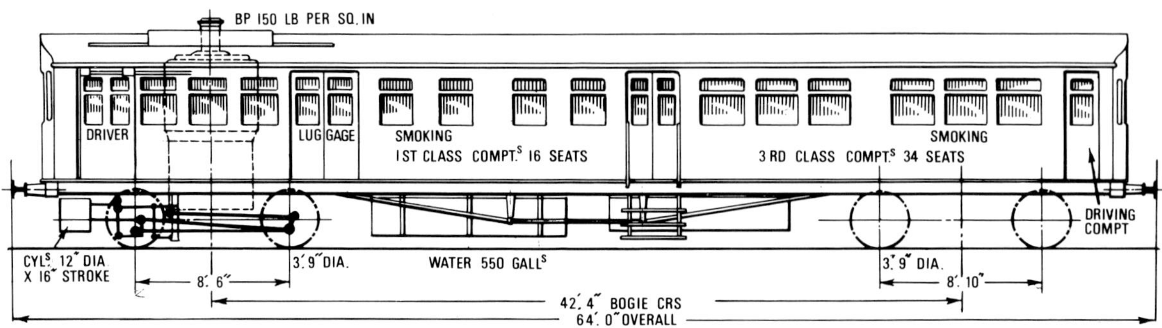

Above: The disposition of equipment is quite well shown in this side view of the GCR petrol-electric car, with the engine within the coach body, and the power bogie at the opposite end. On the roof stands the silencer and long radiator. By and large the car was reasonably successful and was capable of hauling a trailer coach. *LPC*

Left: GCR Steam railcar No 3, with seats for 16 first and 34 third class passengers. The cylinders were 12in by 16in, and the water capacity was 550gal. The vertical boiler had a working pressure of 150lb/sq in, and the heating surface totalled 610.36sq ft, being made up from a tube heating surface of 558.0sq ft and a firebox heating surface of 52.36sq ft. The grate area was 13sq ft.

about non-steam propulsion lead to the building of a petrol-electric vehicle in 1912, by the British Westinghouse Electric & Manufacturing Co. It was a compact double bogie car with seating for 50 passengers in two saloons, entered from a central vestibule, and it was quite a good looking vehicle, although the roof was dominated by the silencer and a large radiator. The engine and generator were placed in a compartment behind one of the driving cabs. The fuel capacity was sufficient for 150 miles and the maximum speed was 40mph, with the six-cylinder engine developing 90hp and the generator 55kw, supplying two motors on one of the bogies. A smaller petrol engine powered a vacuum exhaust and train lighting generator.

The GCR General Manager Sam Fay, was extremely enthusiastic about the petrol-electric vehicle and seems to have hoped that this design could sweep steam away from local passenger work, an ideal rather ahead of its time! After initial trials in the Manchester area, the car normally worked in the London area, often hauling an additional six-wheeled composite passenger carriage. It finished its life in 1935 as LNER No 51907, working between Marple and Macclesfield.

2 Named Locomotives

Engines were named when new unless otherwise stated

GREAT CENTRAL RAILWAY:

4-4-0 Class 11B (LNER D9)
(See Section 3)

104	*Queen Alexandra* (c. 1910)
110	*King George V* (1911)
1014	*Sir Alexander*[1] (1902)
1021	*Queen Mary* (1913)

4-4-2 Classes 8D and 8E (LNER C5)
(See Section 8)

258	*The Rt Hon Viscount Cross, GCB, GCSI* (1909)
259	*King Edward VII* (1906)
364	*Lady Henderson*[2] (1907)
365	*Sir William Pollitt* (1907)

4-6-0 Class 8F (LNER B4)
(See section 9)

1097	*Immingham*

4-6-0 Class 1 (LNER B2)
(See Section 15)

423	*Sir Sam Fay*
424	*City of Lincoln*
425	*City of Manchester*
426	*City of Chester*
427	*City of London*[3]
428	*City of Liverpool*

4-6-0 Class 1A (LNER B8)
(See Section 16)

4	*Glenalmond*
279	*Earl Kitchener of Khartoum*
439	*Sutton Nelthorpe*
446	*Earl Roberts of Kandahar*

4-4-0 Class 11E (LNER D10)
(See Section 17)

429	*Sir Alexander Henderson*[4]
430	*Purdon Vicars*
431	*Edwin A. Beazley*

432	*Sir Edward Fraser*
433	*Walter Burgh Gair*
434	*The Earl of Kerry*
435	*Sir Clement Royds*
436	*Sir Berkeley Sheffield*
437	*Charles Stuart-Wortley*[5]
438	*Worsley Taylor*

4-6-0 Class 9P (LNER B3)
(See Section 19)

| 1164 | *Earl Beatty* |
| 1165 | *Valour* |

Below: Sad to relate, the majority of Robinson's locomotive designs were withdrawn at a time when preservation was almost unheard of. As a result some truly beautiful engines have gone forever. At the eleventh hour the BTC realised the need to rescue some permanent record of the great man's work, and Gorton restored this engine. Some details date from later LNER days and the lettering on the tender can be criticised for being too large, but these are minor points. GCR No 506 *Butler-Henderson* is seen immediately after restoration, and shows a typical Robinson nameplate. *British Rail*

1166	*Earl Haig*[6]
1167	*Lloyd George*[7]
1168	*Lord Stuart of Wortley*
1169	*Lord Faringdon*

4-4-0 Class 11F (LNER D11)
(See Section 17)

501	*Mons*
502	*Zeebrugge*
503	*Somme*
504	*Jutland*
505	*Ypres*
506	*Butler-Henderson*
507	*Gerard Powys Dewhurst*
508	*Prince of Wales*
509	*Prince Albert*
510	*Princess Mary*
511	*Marne*

The undermentioned locomotives[8] built by the LNER were named in 1925-26:

6378	*Bailie MacWheeble*
6379	*Baron of Bradwardine*
6380	*Evan Dhu*
6381	*Flora MacIvor*
6382	*Colonel Gardiner*
6383	*Jonathan Oldbuck*
6384	*Edie Ochiltree*
6385	*Luckie Mucklebackit*
6386	*Lord Glenallan*
6387	*Lucy Ashton*
6388	*Captain Craigengelt*
6389	*Haystoun of Bucklaw*
6390	*Hobbie Elliott*
6391	*Wizard of the Moor*
6392	*Malcolm Graeme*
6393	*The Fiery Cross*
6394	*Lord James of Douglas*
6395	*Ellen Douglas*
6396	*Maid of Lorn*
6397	*The Lady of the Lake*
6398	*Laird of Balmawhapple*
6399	*Allan Bane*
6400	*Roderick Dhu*
6401	*James Fitzjames*

[1] Name removed 1913.
[2] Renamed *Lady Faringdon*.
[3] Name removed 1937.
[4] Renamed *Sir Douglas Haig* in 1917 and *Prince Henry* in 1920.
[5] Renamed *Prince George*.
[6] Name removed 1943.
[7] Name removed 1923.
[8] These engines had the name painted on the splasher in shaded sanserif lettering; a tradition perpetuated in their final BR days.

Bibliography

During the research and compilation of this work, the authors have found the following books of valuable assistance, and they are recommended to the reader in search of further information about J. G. Robinson and his locomotives, and about the Great Central Railway:

Great Central Railway (Vols 1, 2, 3), G. Dow
National Railway Museum records
Locomotives of the LNER (various parts), RCTS
Railway Magazine
Railway Observer
Journal of the SLS

Below: The sheer grace and symmetry of a Robinson Atlantic, the famous 'Jersey Lily', is beautifully portrayed in this study of Class 8B 4-4-2 No 362 at the head of the down 12.15 Sheffield express.   *LPC*

1
GREAT CENTRAL